JOHANNES KEPLER:

Life and Letters

JOHANNES KEPLER

The rare portrait by Jacob van der Heyden, member of a
well known family of artists and contemporary of Kepler

JOHANNES KEPLER:
Life and Letters

BY
CAROLA BAUMGARDT
WITH AN INTRODUCTION BY
ALBERT EINSTEIN

PHILOSOPHICAL LIBRARY
NEW YORK

To

DOROTHY CANFIELD FISHER
on her seventieth birthday
in admiration and lasting gratitude

CONTENTS

PREFACE

The biography of Kepler which I herewith offer
to the English reading public is the most detailed
of this kind as yet presented. As far as I can see,
even the modern German biographers have not yet
based their sketches on a full evaluation of the
standard edition of *Johannes Kepler in seinen
Briefen* by Max Caspar and Walther von Dyck,
München und Berlin 1930, 2 vols. Verlag R.
Oldenbourg.

Apart from this basic work, use has been made of
the uncompleted great new Kepler edition by von
Dyck and the old still valuable edition by Christian
Frisch. Further, all the rich literature available in
the Library of Congress has been consulted, though
not always relied on. For all the many services
which the staff of the Congressional Library has
rendered me during the long time needed for the
preparation of this manuscript, I wish to express
my special thanks.

I am much indebted to Mrs. Angelica Canfield
for her kind, efficient help in proofreading and for
very valuable comments.

My warmest thanks, also, to Dr. Herbert Weissberger of Washington Square College and the Heineman Foundation, for providing me with photostats of Kepler manuscripts hitherto unpublished and giving me the permission to show a page in the present work.

Last but not least, I owe special gratitude to Mr. Joseph Frank and Mrs. Rachel Frank for their never tiring help in correcting and remodelling the English of my manuscript.

Needless to say, I am particularly indebted to Albert Einstein who was kind enough to write an introduction to my book.

CAROLA BAUMGARDT

INTRODUCTION

One can only feel grateful that the letters of this incomparable man have been made accessible to an English reading public by Mrs. Baumgardt's translation. The letters extend over a period of time from 1596 to 1631. The selection is governed, primarily, by the necessity of communicating to the reader a picture of Kepler the man as a personality; no attempt is made to bring to the foreground his scientific achievements and their unique consequences. But a reader who knows the state of science at that time can also learn something valuable, in this respect, from these letters.

There we meet a finely sensitive person, passionately dedicated to the search for a deeper insight into the essence of natural events, who, despite internal and external difficulties, reached his loftily-placed goal. Kepler's life was devoted to the solution of a double problem. The sun and the planets alter their apparent position, with relation to the background of the fixed stars, in a complicated manner, accessible to immediate observation; what had been observed and recorded with great diligence, therefore, was not actually the movements of the planets in space but the temporal alterations which the direction earth-planet undergoes during the passage of time. Since Copernicus had persuaded the small group of those competent to judge that the sun, in this process, should be considered as motionless, while the planets—including the earth—should be considered as moving around the sun, the first great problem that presented itself was: the determination of the true movements of the planets, including the earth, as it would look to an observer established on the nearest fixed star, and completely equipped with a stereoscopic double-telescope. This was Kepler's first great problem. The second problem lay in the question: What are the mathematical laws controlling these movements? Clearly, the solution of the second problem, if it were possible for the human spirit to accomplish it, presupposed the solution of the first. For one must first know an event before one can test a theory related to this event.

Underlying Kepler's solution of the first problem is an idea of true genius, which made possible the determination of the true pattern of the earth's course. To be able to construct the earth's course, one needs, besides the sun, a second stable point in planetary space; having such a point, one can—

by employing it and the sun as fixed points for the measurement of angles—determine the true pattern of the earth's course by the same method of triangulation generally used in drawing maps. Where, however, can such a fixed point be found, since all visible objects outside the sun, as a single object, execute unknown movements? Kepler's answer: We know, with great exactitude, the ostensible movement of the planet Mars and the time it takes to circle the sun ("Mars-Year"). Each time that a Mars-Year passes, Mars should be at the same place in (planetary) space. If one limits oneself chiefly to the use of such points of time, the planet Mars represents for these a stable point in planetary space, which may be used as a fixed point in triangulation.

Using this principle, Kepler first determined the true movement of the earth in planetary space. And since the earth itself can be used at any time as a triangulation-point, he was also able to determine by observation the true movements of the other planets.

In this way, Kepler won the foundation for the determination of the three fundamental laws that will remain linked to his name for all time. How much inventive power, how much tireless, obstinate work was necessary to reveal these laws, and to establish their certainty with great precision—naturally, can hardly be evaluated by anyone.

This is what the reader must know, when he sees from the letters under what conditions of personal hardship Kepler completed his gigantic work. Neither by poverty, nor by incomprehension of the contemporaries who ruled over the conditions of his life and work, did he allow himself to be crippled or discouraged. In addition, he dealt with a field of knowledge that immediately endangered the adherent of religious truth. He belonged, nevertheless, to those few who cannot do otherwise than openly acknowledge their convictions on every subject. Nor was he one of those who derive instinctive pleasure from the battle with others, as, for example, was obviously the case with Galileo, whose heavenly maliciousness, even today, delights the understanding reader. Kepler was a pious Protestant, who made no secret of the fact that he did not approve all decisions of the Church; he was, for this reason, looked on as a sort of moderate heretic, and treated accordingly. This leads me to the internal difficulties already touched on that Kepler had to conquer. They are less easy to perceive than the external ones. His life work was possible only when he succeeded in freeing himself to a large extent from the spiritual tradition in which he was born. It was not only a question of religious tradition based on the authority of the Church, but of the general notions about the conditioning of events in the cosmos and in human life, as well as ideas about the relative importance of thought and experience in science.

He had to free himself from an animistic, teleologically oriented manner of thinking in scientific research. He had to realize clearly that logical-mathematical theoretizing, no matter how lucid, could not guarantee truth by itself; that the most beautiful logical theory means nothing in natural science without comparison with the exactest experience. Without this philosophic attitude, his work would not have been possible. He does not speak about this, but the inner struggle is reflected in the letters. The reader should note the remarks on astrology. They show that the inner enemy, conquered and rendered innocuous, was not yet completely dead. ALBERT EINSTEIN

Princeton, New Jersey

YOUTH AND YEARS OF
APPRENTICESHIP

How little does the educated man of our time know about Johannes Kepler! Generally, even astronomers know only that Kepler, the German, was, probably, the most highly gifted among the four great founders of modern physics and astronomy—the heir and executor of the ideas of Copernicus, the Pole, the friend and collaborator of the great Italian Galileo Galilei and the most important of the forerunners of Isaac Newton, the first systematizer of modern science.

It is, however, hardly common knowledge that Kepler was not only one of the greatest scientific geniuses of all times, but also something of a poet and one of the most lovable and moving personalities of modern history. The nobility and superiority of character with which he endured a life full of hardship is still a shining example of inner spiritual strength in the midst of outward failure.

Max Brod, the fine poet, friend and editor of Franz Kafka, has written an exquisite novel dealing with the youth of Kepler and his relation to his teacher and collaborator, Tycho Brahe, whose astronomical teaching he was destined to outshine. The novel has been translated into English under the title *The Redemption of Tycho Brahe*. It gives a very valuable insight into the thoughts and feelings of the young Kepler.

But nowhere is full justice done to the man's bitter, stirring, lifelong struggle with a grim fate, and the striking inner victories of his gay and warmhearted nature over all the darkness of the circumstances that surrounded him. This fight for truth and personal integrity did not end until death came to him in his sixtieth year of life.

Everyone takes it for granted today that the paradoxical theory of Copernicus is scientifically superior to the common sense belief in the movements of the sun around the earth. We are no longer aware of how heretic, how absurd and how dangerous the Copernican theory was thought to be in the sixteenth and seventeenth centuries. We react as narrow-mindedly and unimaginatively as a daughter who found it too difficult to get the right marital partner while she believed it only too simple for her mother to marry her father—so well known to the mother and even the daughter herself.

The "strange" Copernican theory of the movements of the earth around the sun which received its most vital verification in Kepler's life work was in his day generally considered as fantastic nonsense, and as wanton, completely unjustifiable contempt of Biblical teaching and common sense. Kepler had to spend the energies of his genius in an epic struggle for a most paradoxical and difficult truth; and although the subject matter may change from century to century, the life experience of the boldest discoverers of truth, unfortunately, even today, is too often extremely similar to that of Kepler.

Sir David Brewster, the eminent Scottish physicist, rightly counted Kepler among "The great Martyrs of Science";[1] and Goethe rather reduced to banality the fate of Kepler by using him as an illustration for the axiom that the able man overcomes all obstacles in life.[2] Kepler's "martyrdom," however, took place despite the fact that hardly anyone could consider Kepler as an inferior mind during his lifetime, and that posterity was soon to recognize his full genius. Kant saw in him

[1] See D. Brewster, *The Martyrs of Science,* London, n.d. [1888].
[2] *Goethe's Werke,* Weimar, II. Abteilung, vol. III, "Zur Farbenlehre," Historischer Teil I, p. 248.

"the most acute thinker ever born." [3] Johann Gott-
fried von Herder,[4] another of the German classi-
cists of the eighteenth century, emphasized that
Kepler was not only the discoverer of new astronomical truths but also the founder of whole new
branches of sciences. And Alexander von Humboldt,[5] himself a great explorer of nature, has per-
tinently pointed to that "almost unparalleled" combination of bold imaginative power with "mathematical profoundness" which characterizes the
originality of Kepler's mind.

Nor was Kepler himself unaware of the greatness
of his achievements. In the preface of the fifth
chapter of his "Cosmic Harmonies" Kepler con-
cludes his humble apologies for the revolutionary
and allegedly irreligious character in his teaching
with the following proud and exalted sentence:
"Eighteen months ago the first dawn rose for me,

[3] E.A.C. Wasianski, *Immanuel Kant in seinen letzten Lebens-
jahren,* Königsberg, 1804, p. 97.

[4] See J. G. Herder *"Adrastea,"* Band III, Zweites Stück, 1802,
II. "Wissenschaften, Ereignisse und Charaktere des vergangenen
Jahrhunderts," p. 318, in *Herders Sämmtliche Werke,* ed. by Bern-
hard Suphan, Berlin, vol. 23, 1885, p. 549.

[5] A. von Humboldt, *Cosmos,* translated by E. C. Otté, 1852,
p. 327.

three months ago the bright day, and a few days
ago the full sun of a most wonderful vision; now
nothing can keep me back. I let myself go in
divine rage. I defy the mortals with scorn by an
open confession. I have stolen the golden vessels
of the Egyptians to make out of them a holy
tabernacle for my God, far away from the frontiers
of Egypt. If you pardon me, I will be delighted; if
you are angry with me, I shall bear it. Well then,
the die is cast, I am writing a book for my contemporaries or—it does not matter—for posterity.
It may be that my book will have to wait for its
readers for a hundred years. Has not God himself
waited for six thousand years for some one to con-
template his work with understanding?"

This seemingly presumptuous statement is, in the
mouth of Kepler, and seen in its proper context,
free from false pride in quite a unique way. It is,
in truth, dictated by an almost mystical devotion
to his work and his creator. He feels himself only
a tool, a mouthpiece of God, placing at his service all the seemingly disparate talents which
he combined in a most striking harmony, for he was
at the same time a mystic, a tirelessly accurate
observer, and a mathematician.

What, at a superficial glance, may appear as arrogance is, in fact, nothing but Kepler's exuberant feeling of gratitude to Providence—a gratitude for having chosen him to reveal the hidden beauties of cosmic harmonies by means of his extraordinary talents.

Nature had indeed showered Kepler with as many gifts as Mozart. Again and again, the reader of his letters feels struck by the similarity of the two men's temperament which has also been casually indicated by a recent translator of Kepler's first work of youth. Both these Southern Germans, Kepler and Mozart, were filled with an unshakable serenity in the face of overwhelming odds in life and in the development of their gifts. Kepler and Mozart both knew how to reply when attacked; but they never fought with embitterment. Even when they parried blows most sharply or made their most justified complaints, there is never the slightest trace of resentment. They were both endowed with a gay sense of inner freedom, which allowed them to color even highly vexatious situations around them with a golden tint. And this enviably sublime harmony of their natures reveals itself in the same tender, light but extremely warm and natural attitude which the two men had toward women. They are both full of vibrating erotic life, but at the same time of a rare purity and candor of erotic feeling.

It sounds like one of Mozart's playful arias, dedicated to warmhearted girlish gaiety, when Kepler confesses that he always loved the more "polished, noble, dear, timid and so easily frightened tender sex." And yet, how full of passion and deep compassion is so much else that Kepler and Mozart told us about the suffering and the nobility of feeling of mature womanhood!

Despite their rather disparate fields of activity, in their work, too, Kepler and Mozart reveal the same seldom united gifts: utmost aesthetic grace and charm with intellectual accuracy and precision. There is a radiance of rare beauty, not only in Mozart's world of tones, but also in many reflections and statements of Kepler; and there is exhilarating clarity not only in the exact thinking of Kepler, but also in the musical structure of the great Mozartian compositions.

Johannes Kepler was born on December 27th, 1571 in Weil (called also "Weil die Stadt" or

"Weilerstadt"), at that time a Free City of the "Holy German Empire," later of the Kingdom of Württemberg. This small town to the southwest of Stuttgart has preserved its medieval charm up to the present day, especially around the "Kepler-house." Weil obviously had considerably greater importance in the sixteenth century than in later years. But even as a free city it never played any major part in Germany's political life.

The time into which Kepler was born, was that of a spectacular flowering of European culture. Not only were the foundations of modern exact science laid in these decades. Shakespeare, the poet, was flourishing in England; the painters Brueghel, Rubens and Rembrandt in Holland; Velásquez and El Greco, and the author of *Don Quixote,* Cervantes, in Spain; Descartes, "the father of modern philosophy," in France; the great and profound master of early passion music, Heinrich Schütz, in Germany; and Palestrina, the leading reformer of Church music in Italy, was, at least during the last twenty-three years of his life, a contemporary of Kepler.

Kepler was a seven-months' child, but despite his very delicate health, was in no way spoiled by his mother. Soon after her second son was born, she joined her husband in the Netherlands where the very unsteady man was just taking part in another war. Johannes, however, and his younger brother Heinrich, were taken care of by their grandparents in Weil where the grandfather was burgomaster.

During the first years of his life, the boy's health was often frail. A prolonged attack of smallpox almost deprived him of his eyesight. The visual power of the greatest genius in modern astronomy remained, thus, impaired, *"blöd"* from his earliest youth. As in the case of Beethoven, disease threatened exactly that organ which he most needed for the great vocation to which he was called.

Johannes attended the grammar school in Weil until 1577, when he was able to attend the Latin school in Leonberg, another small Swabian town, to which his parents had gone after the Dutch-Spanish war. After having passed his first rather dreaded examination he was sent to the Convent School of Adelberg in 1584. In this school, near the Hohenstaufen—the ancestral castle of the most famous family of the German Emperors of the Middle Ages—the students had to rise daily at 4 o'clock in the morning and to start their days

with psalm singing. The rigid discipline of this
school, as well as renewed attacks of disease and
the envy of a classmate, made these years of
Kepler's youth rather joyless. His health improved
only during the attendance of the higher Convent
School at Maulbronn, a place which only half a
century earlier was haunted by the ill-famed Dr.
Faustus, the magician and hero of the many Faust-
poems in world literature. In these years, up to
1589, when he was admitted to the Swabian University of Tübingen, Kepler acquired his great
mastery of the Latin language, which was later,
rightly, so often praised. Latin verses of his had
already been printed when he was still a student
in Tübingen.

The University of Tübingen, and particularly its
theological seminary, the "Tübinger Stift," belongs
to the most renowned centers of German learning.
Founded in 1477, it was still in the nineteenth century the seat of an internationally famous group of
scholars and teachers, especially the "Tübinger
Schule" of modern critical theologians; and exactly two hundred years after Kepler, the "Tübinger Stift" harbored within its walls three famous
Swabian students, the philosophers Hegel and

Schelling and one of the greatest poets of modern times, Friedrich Hölderlin.

Even as a young student in Tübingen, Kepler was physically so little developed, completely beardless and of such tender stature that he was generally elected to play a woman's part in the dramatic performances in the University. But he played with so much fire and skill that he is reported to have scored special successes. Kepler studied mainly theology and philosophy, but also mathematics and astronomy; and almost up to the end of his life he kept in contact with two of his teachers, the theologian Matthias Hafenreffer and the astronomer Michael Mästlin. With the light flourish of expression popular in those times, but nevertheless with great sincerity, Kepler affirmed later that his teacher Mästlin remained the "living source of the stream which watered his fields." For, although publicly Mästlin was obliged to teach astronomy according to Ptolemy's theory of the sun's movement around the earth, it was obviously Mästlin who led the young Kepler to a firm conviction of the superiority of the Copernican heliocentric astronomy over the old Ptolemaic one.

When Kepler had completed his studies in Tübingen, the University urgently recommended him, early in 1594, for a professorship of Morals and Mathematics at the Protestant "Gymnasium" in Graz, the faraway capital of Styria in Austria. For, although the young Kepler was thought by the Tübingen faculty to be of blameless character and of great intellectual abilities, he was not considered orthodox enough for a Church position in Swabia. In his work *The New Astronomy* (*Astronomia nova*, 1609) Kepler himself later related that at first he was by no means enthusiastic about being sent away to Graz as a teacher in mathematics. For he had prepared himself for a theological pulpit, and had hoped to serve the orthodox Lutheran Church of the country in which he had grown up. But he yielded to the advice given to him by his teachers in Tübingen, and soon the young professor—aged only 21—gained considerable popularity in Graz. The attendance of lectures on mathematics was not obligatory in the capital of Styria, and only a few students had sufficient interest in the difficult subject matter. Therefore, the new professor was charged also with the delivery of lectures on Virgil and on rhetoric, and he good-naturedly took over all these obligations to the full satisfaction of his superiors.

At the request of the nobility and the cities of Styria, and as their official *"mathematicus,"* he published, in the year of his arrival in Graz, a *Calendarium and Prognosticum* for the year 1495 and, before the end of his stay in Graz, he followed it up with five more. As he was expected to do, he registered in these calendars not only the movements of the celestial bodies but indulged in astrological prophecies. Probably more on the basis of common sense than on astrological speculations, he predicted for the year 1595 unrest among the peasants of Upper Austria and a flight of the Austrians from the invading Turks. Both these prophecies came true and this markedly strengthened the prestige and the authority of the young mathematician, even leading to an increase in salary. But Kepler never took pride in his fame as an astrologist. Astrology, or any prophecy of human fate from the constellation of the stars was to him a definitely inferior and—to a large extent—questionable art. In his *Tertius interveniens* (The Intervening Third),

a writing addressed to Feselius, the physician of the
Margrave Georg Friedrich of Baden, he once called
astrology the "foolish little daughter of the respect-
able, reasonable mother astronomy." And although
he never definitely abjured all astrological beliefs,
his main interest remained always concentrated on
the merely theoretical observations and calculations
of the movements of the stars and not on the "practical" value of astronomical observations for the
prediction of human fate.

Kepler's calendar for the year 1495, however,
was read with great interest not only in Styria but
also in Tübingen. There was some misgiving in
Swabia, though, because Kepler progressively
adopted the calendar reform introduced by Pope
Gregory XIII in 1582. The Senate of the University of Tübingen, however, considered the adop-
tion of the "popish" reform as a weakening of the
independence of the Lutheran Church, and Mästlin was officially instructed to write against any
compliance with the astronomical recommendation
of the Catholic Church. But the young Kepler did
not hesitate to disagree on this point even with
his beloved teacher. In a letter of April 19, 1597,

he frankly disapproved of any resistance to the Pope in this matter and thought it, for many reasons, small-minded to demonstrate Protestant independence of thought by protesting against a most useful reform introduced by the Catholic Church.

MARRIAGE AND FIRST SCHOLARLY ACHIEVEMENTS

Along with the success of his calendars went two other events, which opened to Kepler, in these first years of his stay in Graz, a new world of happiness. He fell in love with a young noblewoman, Barbara Müller von Mühlegg, who, though only twenty-two years old, had already been married twice. But here too, quite a number of obstacles had to be overcome before he could found his own household. The bride and her relatives insisted on documentation showing that the bridegroom was of noble descent. To comply with this demand Kepler undertook the journey home to Swabia— at that time quite an enterprise—and he finally succeeded in obtaining the desired papers. But when he returned to Graz after seven months, opponents of his had meanwhile almost succeeded in dissuading the bride and her parents from the marriage, and only after some definite counterpersuasion did the wedding take place on February 9, 1597.

Far more important to posterity, however, was the second joyful event of these years in Graz:

JOHANNES KEPLER:

Kepler's completion of his first major work, which he proudly called: *"Harbinger of Inquiries concerning the Structure of the Universe and containing the Worldmystery"* (*Prodromus dissertationum cosmographicarum continens mysterium cosmographicum . . .*). This work of his youth already reveals something of the bold flights of his poetical and accurate imagination. Never satisfied with a mere dry observation and registration of facts, from the start of his astronomical career he insists on the necessity of thinking out constructive hypotheses which make the observed celestial phenomena intelligible and presuppose a definite order, beauty and harmony in the life of the cosmos. He calls this approach to science his *a priori* method;[6] and in a touching way he describes how much he owes to this method. The necessity of abandoning theology in favor of astronomy had first caused him great unrest. But now, after having made his first

[6] Briefly speaking, Kepler's and Galileo's a priori method consists of their presuppositions of certain hypotheses concerning the explanations of natural events. To the extent that these hypotheses are expressed in mathematical formulas, the mathematical deductions drawn from these formulas are strictly *i.e.* a priori valid, in contrast to merely empirical observations and generalizations by induction.

*Impensûm mi dolabram tempus fûit et
labor et res;
O curas!operis quäntûm ô surgentis inane!*

*Joannes Keplerûs, Imp: Caj: FERDINANDI II.
Ordi...Strie Sûpr-Anfane Mathematicy,
Scripsi Ulmae ...: Aprilis Anno Aerae Chri
...nianorûm accidentalium M DC XXVII.*

KEPLER'S SIGNATURE

The lines above the signature say in free English translation:

Precious time and labor and expenses wasted!
O sorrows, how much mounting work in vain!

A sample of Kepler's countless astronomical calculations

methodical discoveries, he writes full of enthusi-
asm from Graz to Mästlin in Tübingen in praise
of the divine beauty and order of the universe.

Graz, October 3rd, 1595
. . . You see how near I come to truth. As often
as this happens, how can you doubt that I amply
shed tears! For God knows, this *a priori* method
serves to improve the study of the movements of the
celestial bodies; we can put all our hopes into it if
others cooperate who have observations at their
disposal. . . . I am eager to publish (my observations) soon, not in my interest, dear teacher . . . I
strive to publish them in God's honor who wishes to
be recognized from the book of nature. But the
more others continue in these endeavors, the more
I shall rejoice; I am not envious of anybody. This
I pledged to God, this is my decision. I had the
intention of becoming a theologian. For a long time
I was restless: but now see how God is, by my
endeavors, also glorified in astronomy.

Only a few months later Kepler sent his completed work to his superiors in Styria with the following dedication:

JOHANNES KEPLER:

To the Baron von Herberstein
and the Estates of Styria

Graz, May 15, 1596

What I promised seven months ago, a work
which, according to the testimony of the scholars, is
beautiful and appealing and by far superior to the
yearly calendar—this I at last bring before the
high circle, illustrious gentlemen; a work which,
though small in size and accomplished with not
too much trouble, yet deals with a most wonderful
object . . . two thousand years ago Pythagoras[7]
had already tried his hand at it. Does one desire
something new? For the first time I make this subject generally known to mankind. Does one desire
something of importance? Nothing is greater and
larger than the universe. Does one desire something
of dignity? Nothing is more precious, nothing more
beautiful than our bright Temple of God. Does one
want to gain mystical insight? Nothing in nature
is or was more mysterious and more deeply hidden.

[7] According to Simplicius' commentary on Aristotle's *De caelo*
(book II. 9, 290b, 291a) ed. by Simon Karsten, 1865, p. 208b f,
the Greek philosopher Pythagoras of Samos (about 500 B.C.)
spoke of a harmony of heavenly spheres. He and even more his
followers about 400 B.C. put special emphasis on the use of mathematics in the exploration of nature.

There is only one reason why my subject will not interest all and everybody: its value will not appeal to the thoughtless. Here is treated the Book of Nature which is so highly praised by the Holy Scriptures. Paul presents it to the heathens so that they may see God in it just as the sun can be observed in water or a mirror. Why should we Christians take less pleasure in contemplating this since it is our task to honor God in the right way, to worship and admire Him? Our worship is all the more deep, the more clearly we recognize the creation and its greatness. Indeed how many songs did David sing, the true servant to the true God! He received the idea for his songs from the admiring observation of the skies. "The heavens declare the glory of God," he says. . . .

I do not want to stress that I present important evidence of the creation of the universe—an evidence which has been denied by the philosophers. Nevertheless here we see how God, like a human architect, approached the founding of the world according to order and rule and measured everything in such a manner, that one might think not art took nature for an example but God Himself, in the course of His creation took the art of man as an example, though man was to appear only later on.[8]

Must one measure the value of the heavenly object with dimes as one does food? But, pray, one will ask, what is the good of the knowledge of nature, of all astronomy, to a hungry stomach? . . . Painters are allowed to go on with their work because they give joy to the eyes, musicians because they bring joy to the ears, though they are of no other use to us. . . . What insensibility, what stupidity, to deny the spirit an honest pleasure but permit it to the eyes and ears! He who fights against this joy fights against nature. . . . Should . . . the kind creator who brought forth nature out of nothing . . . deprive the spirit of man, the master of creation and the Lord's own image, of every heavenly delight? Do we ask what profit the little bird hopes for in singing? We know that singing in itself is a joy to him because he was created for singing. We must not ask therefore why the human spirit takes such trouble to find out the secrets of the skies. Our creator has given us a spirit in addi-

[8] It is an old religious idea expressed especially graphically in a famous Jewish Sabbath song that man was the last object of God's creation but the first in his plan of the creation.

tion to the senses, for another reason than merely to provide a living for ourselves. Many types of living creatures, in despite of the unreasonableness of their souls, are capable of providing for themselves more ably than we. But our creator wished us to push ahead from the appearance of the things which we see with our eyes to the first causes of their being in growth, although this may be of no immediate practical avail to us. The other creatures and the body of man are kept alive by taking food and drink. But man's soul is something quite different from the other part of man, and the soul is kept alive, enriched and grows by that food called knowledge. The man who does not long for these things is therefore more of a corpse than a living being. Now nature sees to it that there is no shortage of food for the living beings. We are therefore well justified in saying that the variety of the phenomena of nature is so great, the hidden treasures in the dome of the universe so rich, that nature should never run short in material for the human spirit, that the human spirit . . . ought never come to rest, but that there should be always in this world a workshop open for the training of man's spirit. . . . To the astronomer one glory is recompense enough, that he writes his work for the wise men, not for the town criers, for the kings and not for the shepherds. I proclaim without hesitation that there are human beings who will draw comfort from this fact in their old age, men who after having accomplished their public work will be able to enjoy these pleasures with a free conscience.

Yes, there will appear one day a Charles V, who as a master of Europe could not find what later, tired of ruling, he found in the small cell of St. Yuste. In the midst of all other festivities, titles, triumphs, riches, towns and kingdoms, he will have so much joy of the Pythagorean . . . or . . . Copernican planetary spheres, that he will exchange the whole world for them and, rather than rule peoples with the scepter, he will choose to rule the celestial spheres with measuring instruments. . . .

Written on the 15th of May on which, one year ago, I started this work.

The astronomical hypotheses developed in Kepler's youthful work can no longer be upheld. Kepler himself later broke completely away from the belief that the orbits of the planets are circles—

a thesis he had developed in the *Mysterium*. Thirteen years later it was he who, in his *Astronomia nova*, 1609, firmly laid the foundations of modern exact astronomy by the hypothesis that the orbits of the planets are ellipses in whose one focus the sun is situated (the so-called first Kepler Law). Also, the other speculations of the *Mysterium* concerning the role of the five regular polygons in astronomy were later abandoned by Kepler himself. And yet, even those first tentative suggestions of his *Mysterium cosmographicum* of 1596 rightly impressed the leading scientists of the time—such as the Dane Tycho Brahe, the Italian Galileo and others—by their mathematical imaginativeness. Mästlin wrote in a testimonial to the Prorector Hafenreffer of the University of Tübingen in June 1596: "The topic and the ideas (of Kepler's *Mysterium cosmographicum*) are so new that up to now they never entered anybody's mind. . . . For who ever conceived the idea or made such daring attempt as to demonstrate *a priori* the number, the order, the magnitude and the movements of the celestial spheres . . . and to elicit all this from the secret, unfathomable decrees of Heaven!" But Mästlin criticized Kepler in detail for having not sufficiently popularized and elucidated his ideas.

Along with other scholars, Galileo Galilei, the great physicist of Italy, also received a copy of Kepler's first major work and immediately after receipt of the book Galileo wrote to his German colleague.

Galileo to Kepler

Padua, August 4th, 1597

Your book, highly learned gentleman, which you sent me through Paulus Amberger, reached me not days ago but only a few hours ago, and as this Paulus just informed me of his return to Germany, I should think myself indeed ungrateful if I should not express to you my thanks by this letter. I thank you especially for having deemed me worthy of such a proof of your friendship. . . . So far I have read only the introduction, but have learned from it in some measure your intentions and congratulate myself on the good fortune of having found such a man as a companion in the exploration of truth. For it is deplorable that there are so few who seek the truth and do not pursue a wrong method of philosophizing. But this is not the place to mourn about the misery of our century but to rejoice with you about such beautiful ideas proving the truth. So I add only this promise that I will read your book in peace, for I am certain that I will find the most beautiful things in it. . . . I would certainly dare to approach the public with my ways of thinking if there were more people of your mind. As this is not the case, I shall refrain from doing so. The lack of time and the ardent wish to read your book make it necessary to close, assuring you of my sympathy. I shall always be at your service. Farewell, and do not neglect to give me further good news of yourself.

Yours in sincere friendship,
Galilaeus Galilaeus
Mathematician at the Academy of Padua

Kepler was obviously much pleased by this letter from Galileo and wrote to Michael Mästlin:

Graz, September 1597
. . . Lately I have sent two copies of my little book to Italy. They were received with gladness by a mathematician named Galileo Galilei, as he

signs himself. He has also been attached for many
years to the Copernican heresy.

To Galileo's letter of August 1597 Kepler re-
plied:

Graz, October 13th, 1597
I received your letter of August 4th on September 1st. It was a double pleasure to me. First,
because I became friends with you, the Italian, and
second because of the agreement in which we find
ourselves concerning Copernican cosmography.
As you invite me kindly at the end of your letter
to enter into correspondence with you, and I myself feel greatly tempted to do so, I will not let pass
the occasion of sending you a letter with the present
young nobleman. For I am sure, if your time has
allowed it, you have meanwhile obtained a closer
knowledge of my book. And so a great desire has
taken hold of me, to learn your judgment. For this
is my way, to urge all those to whom I have written
to express their candid opinion. Believe me, the
sharpest criticism of one single understanding man
means much more to me than the thoughtless ap-
plause of the great masses.

I would, however, have wished that you who
have such a keen insight [into everything] would
choose another way [to reach your practical aims.]
By the strength of your personal example you
advise us, in a cleverly veiled manner, to go out
of the way of general ignorance and [warn us
against exposing ourselves to] the furious attacks of
the scholarly crowd. (In this you are following the
lead of Plato and Pythagoras, our true masters.)
But after the beginning of a tremendous enterprise
has been made in our time, and furthered by so
many learned mathematicians, and after the statement that the earth moves can no longer be regarded as something new, would it not be better
to pull the rolling wagon to its destination with
united effort. . . . For it is not only you Italians
who do not believe that they move unless they feel
it, but we in Germany, too, in no way make ourselves popular with this idea. Yet there are ways in
which we protect ourselves against these difficulties.
. . . Be of good cheer, Galileo, and appear in
public. If I am not mistaken there are only a few
among the distinguished mathematicians of Europe
who would dissociate themselves from us. So great
is the power of truth. If Italy seems less suitable for

your publication and if you have to expect difficulties there, perhaps Germany will offer us more freedom. But enough of this. Please let me know, at least privately if you do not want to do so publicly, what you have discovered in favor of Copernicus.

Now I want to ask you for an observation; as I possess no instruments I must turn to other people. Do you possess a quadrant which shows minutes and quarterminutes? If so, then, please, observe at about the time of the 19th of December the smallest and the largest altitude of the middle star of the tail in the great dipper. Likewise observe about December 26th both heights of the polar star. Also observe the first star about the 19th of March 1598 in its height at midnight, the second about September 28th, also around midnight. If, as I wish, there could be shown a difference between the two observations of one or another minute or even 10′ to 15′, this would be proof of something of great importance for all astronomy. If there is no difference shown, however, we shall earn all the same together the fame of having become aware of an important problem hitherto not noticed by anybody. [Fixed-star parallax]. . . . Farewell and answer me with a very long letter.

Obviously, in these first years in Graz, Kepler was still so full of optimism and confident of friendly approval in the scholarly world that he could make a concerted effort to win over the far more sceptical Galileo to the same hope of educating the public to their ideas.

But very soon, the horizon of his life darkened. The growing pressure of the Counter Reformation was felt by Kepler as early as in the spring of 1598, when he reported it in a letter to Mästlin. Nevertheless, he bore all this, and even the death of the children born to him in Graz, with great self-control. The letters of these years mainly show a full concentration on his extensive research interests.

To Herwart [9]

Graz, March 26th, 1598

. . . You think from the winds and the movements of the oceans one could deduce reasons for

[9] Johann Georg Herwart von Hohenburg (1553–1622) was a Bavarian statesman, jurist, historian and mathematician.

the movement of the earth. I too have some ideas concerning these things. Galileo, a mathematician of Padua, assured me that he could quite correctly derive from the Copernican hypothesis the origin of very many natural phenomena which could not be explained by common hypotheses of others, though he did not mention details. On this occasion I also thought of the tides. Reflecting on these phenomena, it seems to me that we must not exclude the moon so far as we can deduce from it the calculation of the tides, and I think we can do that. He who ascribes the movement of the oceans to the movement of the earth refers to a forced movement; but he who lets the oceans follow the moon, in a certain way makes this movement a natural one. . . . In short, the hypotheses are not new but the ways of using them are new; they are a mixture of the old hypotheses with the new ones of Copernicus. I think thus: as we astronomers are priests of the highest God in regard to the book of nature, we are bound to think of the praise of God and not of the glory of our own capacities. Who is convinced of that does not publish light-mindedly what he does not believe himself. . . . I am content with the honor of having my discovery guard the doors of the sanctuary in which Copernicus performs the service at the higher altar. . . .

In a letter to Mästlin of the same year, Kepler describes with special sympathy the joy of discovery experienced by ancient mathematicians.

Graz, June 11th, 1598

. . . I want to mention some ancient mathematicians and the joy their inventions gave them. They are related by Petrus Ramus, whom I have read recently, in his *Scholae mathematicae*.[10] . . .

(1) THALES, one of the seven sages of Greece, after discovering how *latus trianguli* (the side of the triangle) compares with *diametro circumscripti circuli* (diameter of the circumscribed circle), took

---

[10] Petrus Ramus (Pierre de La Ramé), born about 1515, a French logician and humanist, was sometimes thought to have been the predecessor of Descartes. He was involved in a famous controversy with the Aristotelians of the Sorbonne and being a convert to Protestantism he was assassinated two days after the massacre of St. Bartholomew (1572). His *Scholarum mathematicarum libri unus et triginta*, to which Kepler refers here, appeared in Basle in 1569. Even in the last years of his life, John Milton was so much interested in Ramé's logic that he published a compendium of it in 1672.

it for such a great kindness of the Gods that he sacrificed an ox in gratitude to the Muses.

(2) PYTHAGORAS, the grandfather of all Copernicans, who doubtlessly had more intellectual power than the German mathematicians, did about the same. When he discovered the comparableness of *subtensae et laterum rectanguli* (hypotenuse and the sides of a right-angled triangle), which contains one of the fundamentals of geometry—he sacrificed a hundred oxen.

(3) ERATOSTHENES promised gratitude to the Gods if he could solve the knotty question *de duplicando cubo* (on the duplication of the cube). And when he succeeded in some measure, he erected a tablet on which he indicated his discovery and had it put up publicly in one of the God's temples. He also wrote a letter to Ptolemy, King of Egypt, in which he praised and commended the high art to him.

(4) ARCHIMEDES reflected long and thoroughly. . . . He ordered that after his death his glorious invention of the comparableness of *globi et cylindri* (globe and cylinder) should be put on his tombstone: which, in fact, was done. . . .

. . . About the death of your little son I mourn with you the more as I can judge the greatness of your grief by my own sorrow. For the all-merciful God has called my little son Heinrich just at the time when, as I wrote you, I most feared for him. . . . No day can diminish my wife's painful longing for him. . . . My heart is heavy with the thought "O vanity of vanities and everything is vanity!" . . .

My countrymen maintained that they have seen at times Venus as a comet [an omen of threat and disaster]. When asked about it, I said that, according to my opinion, there is no milder star in the heavens. . . .

To Mästlin

Graz, December 9th, 1598

. . . The reason for my writing so little about the eclipses was my compilation of the calendar which I herewith present to you. Forgive me, my best teacher. There is much I must apologize for or it would damage my reputation in your eyes. The matter is this: in this calendar I do not write for the large crowd nor for scholars (with a few exceptions) but for noblemen and the prelates, who pretend to have a knowledge about things which they do not understand. . . . I have only one thing in mind, to turn to my advantage the truth of which I am always a willing champion, though I am not always a fit one. As to all the prognoses, I intend to present to my above mentioned readers a pleasant enjoyment of the grandeur of nature along with the statements which appear true to me, . . . thus hoping that the readers may be tempted to approve a raise in my salary, which has not yet been increased, just as my expenses have not yet been refunded. If you agree with this you will, I hope, not be angry with me if as a defender of astrology in word and action, at the same time I try to implant the opinion in the masses that I am not an astrological buffoon. This I have done this year. . . .

Suggestions for explaining the Copernican idea

To Herwart

Graz, December 16, 1598

. . . Copernicus . . . piously exclaimed with astonishment and admiration: "So great indeed is the edifice of our Almighty and Allkind Creator."

And yet, it is no little consolation to reflect that we should feel less astonished at the huge and almost endless width of the heavens than at the smallness of us human beings, the smallness of this, our tiny ball of earth, and all the planets. The world is not immeasurable to God; but to God we are puny, compared with this world. . . . Yet one must not infer from bigness to special importance. For God who lives above, still looks down at the humble. If the planets were the most unimportant part of the world because the entire planetary system practically disappears when compared with the fixed star system, according to this same argument man would belong to the absolute trifles in the world, since he can in no way be compared with the earth and this, the earth, in turn cannot be compared with the world of Saturn. Yes, the crocodile or the elephant would be closer to God's heart than man, because these animals surpass the human being in size. With these and other sugar-coatings on the pill, maybe, this huge morsel could be digested.

On science in general and on his own character he writes to Herwart:

JOHANNES KEPLER:

Graz, 9th and 10th of April, 1599
. . . To God there are, in the whole material
world, material laws, figures and relations of special excellency and of the most appropriate order.
. . . Let us therefore not try to discover more of
the heavenly and immaterial world than God has
revealed to us. Those laws are within the grasp of
the human mind; God wanted us to recognize
them by creating us after his own image so that we
could share in his own thoughts. For what is there
in the human mind besides figures and magnitudes?
It is only these which we can apprehend in the
right way, and if piety allows us to say so, our
understanding is in this respect of the same kind as
the divine, at least as far as we are able to grasp
something of it in our mortal life. Only fools fear
that we make man godlike in doing so; for the
divine counsels are impenetrable, but not his material creation.

The philosophical pearls picked out of Ara-
bian trifles concern the material which Aristotle
treated in his books *On Coming to Be and Passing
Away* and the *Phaenomena in the Air*. I presented
part of this material in the introduction to my
calendar of this year, which is in your hands. . . .

I mention only some of these items by way of questions.

How is it that all humidity has some connection with the light of the moon? Why do the tides of the seas follow the movements of the fireballs in the skies? In which way can a constellation be effective and why not every constellation but only a rational one? . . . Another question: how does the face of the sky affect the character of man at the moment of his birth? It affects the human being as long as he lives in no other way than the knots which the peasant haphazardly puts around the pumpkin. They do not make the pumpkin grow but decide its shape. So does the sky; it does not give the human being morals, happiness, children, fortune and wife, but it shapes everything in which the human being is engaged. And yet, from the constellation of birth during the course of a human life, the sky adopts many shapes. It never remains the same. So the constellation at birth is passing. Now, how nevertheless can something be active that does not exist? It is active in so far as it has had that position once. . . . Look at the human being at whose birth the constellation of Jupiter and Venus were not fortunate. You will see that such a human being can be just and wise, but has a less gay and rather sad fate. Such a woman is known to me. [Kepler thinks of his own wife.] She is praised throughout the city on account of virtue, chastity and modesty. But she is simple-minded and stout . . . has difficulties in bearing children. . . . Thus you can recognize in the soul, the body and the fate, the same character; and this is indeed analogous to the constellations in such a way that it is impossible for the soul to be the moulder of its entire fate, because fate is something coming from the outside, something foreign.

With me Saturn and the sun operate together. . . . Therefore my body is dry and knotty, not tall. The soul is faint-hearted, it hides itself in literary nooks; it is distrustful, frightened, seeks its way through tough brambles and is entangled in them. Its moral habits are analogous. To gnaw bones, eat dry bread, taste bitter and spiced things is a delight to me; to walk over rugged paths, uphill, through thickets is a feast and a pleasure to me. I know no other way of seasoning my life than science; I do not long for other spices and reject them if offered to me. My fate is strikingly similar to these statements. Where others despair, a path opens itself before me to fortune and fame, of course not an excessively large one. For, in rising, I am always oppressed. While circumstances change, the form always remains the same. No matter how far I have advanced, I have been strongly opposed everywhere. Perhaps my mind will meet the same fate because challenging mankind I maintain the movement of the earth "pushing on with tightened neck the heavy weight of the earth rapidly through the universe of stars while the assembly of the earth's inhabitants is protesting against it." But this can be considered as the common fate of all distinguished men. Applicable is the saying: "The beautiful is hard to conquer" and that well-known proverb of Cicero: "The Gods have planted sweat before virtue."

Meanwhile Kepler's forebodings of growing religious intolerance in Styria had become more and more justified. During the last two years of the century, Styrian Protestantism was step by step oppressed by decrees of the young Archduke Ferdinand, who had been educated by the Jesuits and had vowed to lead back all his Austrian subjects into the *"Schoss der katholischen Kirche"* (back to the bosom of the Catholic Church). Kepler describes his increasing anxieties about the situation mainly in letters to Mästlin. Toward the end of September 1598, all Protestant theologians and teachers were expelled from Styria and Kepler had to flee to Hungary while his wife was allowed to remain in Graz. Probably on the recommendation of influential friends, and also because of the government's hope that the good-natured conciliatory astronomer could be won over to Catholicism, Kepler was allowed to return to his home after only a month of exile. Nevertheless, he clearly foresaw that the chance of his permanent stay in Graz would grow from bad to worse. After his marriage, he had hoped that the comparatively favorable financial status of his wife's family and his own teaching position would secure for him long years of concentration on his work; and as late as December 1598 he speaks of his wife's and his own great reluctance to leave Styria. But more and more in the course of 1599, he entreats Mästlin to assist him in securing a professorship of philosophy or even medicine at his beloved University of Tübingen. He explains to his former teacher in detail that it is not blind despair or any frivolous desire for a change which drives him away from Graz. He is fully aware of the difficulties he would encounter everywhere outside his present home, even in Tübingen; and he does not forget to mention that he is still shown a good deal of kindness by the "intelligentsia" in Graz. But he insists that, in his opinion, the situation of Protestant teachers in Styria was bound to deteriorate rapidly.

He reports in August 1599 that already everyone who "reads the Bible of Luther" or sings a Protestant choral in Graz, runs the risk of being expelled, or is penalized by a fine or imprisonment; and he rightly prophesied that soon it would even be impossible for emigrants to take any of their possessions from Austria. He therefore asks Mästlin to let him know the price of bread, wine and rent in Tübingen.

Mästlin, however, obviously felt disturbed by these inquiries. He confesses that he is not experienced enough to give proper information on these points and apparently did not respond at all to some further letters of his former student.

Finally, on August 1, 1600, Kepler along with several thousand of Protestant citizens was expelled from Styria forever. He had to pay heavy taxes and to sell all his household goods in great haste and at a very low price, while, as he had foreseen two years earlier, he would have been able to save his possessions if he had not at that time been granted a return from exile. This permission to return was obviously a fatal gift, as he exclaims in a letter of September 19, 1600 addressed to Mästlin; he "who loves his home will lose it"; and in his deep anxiety he writes in the same letter:

". . . I would go to you with my family by boat on the Danube, if God lets me survive. I would start the medical career, if you would perhaps give me an assistant professorship. For indeed, I have become quite poor, after having hoped to become rich one day. I have taken a wife of good fortune; her whole family is in the same boat. Yet all her possessions are invested in real estate and since these have come down in price now, they are hardly marketable. Everybody is lying in wait to get them for nothing. The prince [Ferdinand, Archduke of Austria] has issued the decree that nobody may rent his estates to a follower of the Pope unless these estates are sold within forty-five days."

And then he adds the following moving confession:

"All this is rather hard. But I should not have believed that in the communion of brethren it is so sweet to suffer loss or insult for our faith and Christ's honor, and to abandon home, fields, friends and country. If it is the same with real martyrdom and the sacrifice of life, if the joy is the greater, the greater the loss, then it must also be an easy thing to die for faith. . . ."

Of course Kepler could have gained permission to stay in Styria if he had abjured his adherence to his faith and had become a Catholic. But this evidently never entered his mind. Meanwhile, however, some help came from relatively unexpected quarters. Kepler had corresponded for some years with Johann Georg Herwart von Hohenburg (also a pupil of Mästlin), an influential Bavarian diplomat, strongly interested in science. Apart from astronomical observations which Kepler reported to Herwart, he had also frankly written him—the Catholic—about his religious views: Dec. 16, 1598 "I have accepted . . . the Augsburg confession (the Lutheran articles of faith), and I adhere to it. I have not learned to simulate, I am in earnest with my religion, I don't play with it" and again on May

30, 1599 he writes with similar frankness to Herwart on his attitude toward superstition: "As to the guardian angels I do not wish to engage in any controversy. All this is a matter of opinion and not an object of knowledge. Perhaps one day someone will offer a natural explanation and a reference to guardian angels will no longer be needed. I myself hope to be free from superstition."

At the same time Kepler in his letters frequently asks Herwart to forgive him, and to attribute it to "the moods of the mathematicians" if he had not always used "official language" in his correspondence with such a high official as Herwart was. For "the style of a letter should come from the heart, it must be free." Herwart, in 1600, drew Kepler's attention to a possible collaboration with Tycho Brahe, the greatest astronomical observer of that time. Kepler had already contacted Brahe in 1597 by sending him a copy of his first work, the *Mysterium cosmographicum*. Brahe lived at that time in Wandsbeck near Hamburg, after he had been forced by the intrigues of adversaries to renounce the splendid position he had held for years in Denmark, where his King, Frederick II, had donated a whole island to him and an excellent observatory.

Brahe had immediately recognized the very high qualities of Kepler's youthful work, praised in a letter to him the acuteness of his mind and his "well-rounded way of expression," but wondered whether he could agree with all of Kepler's theses. When, a short time later, Brahe was appointed "Mathematicus of the Imperial Court" in Prague by the German Emperor Rudolph II, Brahe invited Kepler, probably at the suggestion of Herwart, for a visit to his castle, Benatek near Prague. Kepler accepted Tycho's invitation and stayed in Brahe's home from February to June 1600 with the exception of only a few weeks.

A really adequate description both of the inner and outer differences in the relation of these two leading astronomers is certainly an extremely delicate and almost impossible task. There was a marked point of possible friction in the fact that Brahe was an avowed anti-Copernican and is said to have implored his younger collaborator even on his deathbed not to use his life-long observations for the support of the Copernican theory. But there must have also been a strong contrast in temperament and in the whole style of demeanor between the two men which led to misunderstandings and conflicts, starting during the first few months of their cooperation, or even before that time in connection with a polemics of the astronomer Ursus, the assistant of Tycho Brahe. Tycho's letters, as far as preserved, generally betray still a sincere warmth and genuine esteem for his younger colleague, and also the poem which Kepler wrote on the occasion of Tycho's death reveals no less deep affection for his predecessor.

But in all probability, some traits, something in the demeanor of the Danish grandseigneur and his marked pride in his lifework often must have offended Kepler. On the other hand we possess from Kepler's hand a long letter of apologies offered to Tycho, in which he accuses himself in a quite unusual excitement of inexcusable affronts with which he had repaid the hospitality and all the other tokens of friendship shown to him by a scholar of such highest renown and dignity. How far these apologies may be exaggerated in order to conciliate an undue irritability on the part of Tycho is doubtless difficult to determine. In a letter to Herwart, after his return from his first visit to Tycho, Kepler writes:

I would have concluded my research on the harmonies of the world, if Tycho's astronomy had not fascinated me so much that I almost went out of my mind; still I wonder what could be done further in this direction. One of the most important reasons for my visit to Tycho was the desire, as you know, to learn from him more correct figures for the eccentricities in order to examine my *Mysterium* and the just mentioned *Harmony* for comparison. For these speculations *a priori* must not conflict with experimental evidence; moreover they must be in accordance with it. But Tycho did not give me the chance to share his practical knowledge except in conversation during meals, today something about the Apogee, tomorrow something about the knots of another planet.

But when he saw that I possess a daring mind, he thought the best way to deal with me would be to give me my head, to let me choose the observations of one single planet, Mars. This has taken up all my time and I have not been concerned with observations of another planet. I was hoping from day to day for a happy solution concerning the theory of Mars; later I thought I would also get the other observations. . . . Tycho was pleased with these experiments of mine; for a long time, he said, he himself had been occupied with the same ones, but he would like to avoid the complicated calculations and therefore wished to get acquainted with other people's views. . . .

In any case still at the time of his visit to Prague, in spite of the hopeless conditions in Styria, Kepler made efforts to get a university position in Tübingen rather than the position of an assistant to Tycho. Only after practically all his other hopes had vanished he travelled for the second time in the same year to Prague and arrived there with his wife in October 1600. Yet even after his return to Prague he writes to Mästlin on December 16, 1600:

"As I succumbed [on the way from Graz to Prague] to the intermittent fever, I cannot tell you what a paroxysm of melancholy your letter caused me by destroying all my hope of being appointed at your university. Here in Prague everything is uncertain and uncertain with regard to my life, too, but now I must stay here until I either recover or die. Everything is four times more expensive here

than elsewhere. I especially pity my wife who is
with me . . . I entreat you, venerated teacher, to insist on my being appointed [at the University of
Tübingen], as soon as there is any vacancy. I certainly would conduct myself as befits a grateful
pupil. Believe me, if I came to Tübingen many
noble men of Styria who would go to other places
would study there. . . . Tycho philosophizes rather
queerly. Farewell and remember me who lives here
and under unhappy conditions after you have always shown me affection as long as I was happy."

Even a letter early in 1601 does not sound more
cheerful.

To Mästlin
                    Prague, February 8, 1601
    I have nothing to write you, dear teacher, but
to ask you to answer my last letter and to request
from Messrs. Hafenreffer and Ziegler to write me
also . . . for I need consolation. I still suffer from
intermittent fever and from a dangerous cough;
one is afraid that it might be tuberculosis, which is
fatal. Now my wife, too, is ill and during the four
months I have been here I have already spent 100

thaler . . . little money is left. Tycho promises me much. If he could act as he would like to, none would be more satisfied than I. . . . The love of my native country drives me to you, whatever may be the future of my homeland [Mästlin had written Kepler in 1599 that conditions in Württemberg were as bad as everywhere and that all he could do would be to pray for him]. I have gone down once when the world around me collapsed; I have no fear . . . Tycho is very stingy as to communicating his [astronomical] observations. But I am allowed to use them daily. If I could only copy them quickly enough! I must, however, be content with making selections from them and ask you to tell me what, in your opinion, is mainly to be noted and selected. . . . The disease obscures my style in addition to my being sufficiently burdened with the gift of being abstruse. I am not satisfied with myself . . . If you should send him [Tycho] some of your observations, he would, I think, send some to you, too, if you ask him to do so. For in spite of all the instability of his character, he is, after all, a man of great benevolence. All [his observations] are accessible to me but first I had to promise solemnly

to keep them secret. I have complied with this as
far as it befits a philosopher.

But once more and, in fact, for the last time, the
fate of Kepler took a more favorable turn than he
could have expected early in 1601. When Kepler
went for a short business trip to Graz to regain some
of his belongings left there, two letters exchanged
between him and his wife show that their financial
plight was anything but reassuring in 1601; the
proud Mrs. Kepler was waiting for some cash from
Tycho to buy wood for the household. Finally, however, a larger salary was paid to Kepler by the
Imperial Treasury, and when Tycho died in October 1601 Kepler was informed, probably at the
request of Herwart, that the Emperor would make
him Tycho's successor. After he had applied for
the position of the "S. C. M. Mathematicus,"
Mathematician of His Holy Christian Majesty, he
writes to Mästlin:

. . . What the answer will be, time will show. I
myself am full of hope. For, if God has taken care
of what is most important, namely of a subject to

which I can apply my talent, then he will also take care of the necessary money. If, therefore, God has any interest in astronomy, a belief which demands piety, I hope that I shall achieve something in this field, as I see that God has united me with Tycho by an inexorable fate without having disunited us by the most serious misunderstanding. . . . Tycho's main accomplishments are his observations, he has produced just as many magnificent volumes as years given to this work. But also his *Progymnasmata* [11] (in which he treats the fixed stars and the movements of the sun and the moon in our time) really smell of ambrosia. I hope to edit them in time for the next fair. I am working busily on them, making an appendix to them. As far as the moon is concerned, in the last years chiefly, the work of a certain Christian Severin Longomontanus[12] of Denmark has been brought to comple-

[11] Tycho Brahe's *Astronomiae instauratae progymnasmata* appeared first in Copenhagen, 1589, later in Prague, 1602, see Jacques Charles Brunet, *Manuel du libraire et de l'amateur de livres,* Paris, 1860, tome I, p. 1199.

[12] Christian Severin Longomontanus (1562–1647), Danish astronomer, was assistant to Tycho Brahe, 1589–1597, from 1607 Professor of Mathematics in Copenhagen. His controversy with Johann Pell concerning the quadrature of the circle aroused

tion. Tycho kept his hands at the steering wheel in this work. These performances do not show the perfection which is found in the theory of the sun. Tycho wanted to write another book on the comets; he has conducted rather learned and industrious researches on all the planets, somewhat in the fashion of Ptolemy, *mutatis mutandis,* as Copernicus too has done.

Therein you can see how God distributes his gifts; not one of us can do all and everything. Tycho did what Hipparchus did. Their work concerns the foundations of the building. Tycho has thus achieved an immense work. But no single man can do everything. A Hipparchus [13] needs a Ptolemy who builds up the theory of the other five planets. Already during Tycho's lifetime I have achieved this. I have built up a theory of Mars, so that calcu-

---

special interest in the seventeenth century. In 1605 he charged Kepler with untenable innovations and refutations of Tycho's theory of the moon. Kepler answered him with friendliness and superior irony.

[13] Hipparchus of Nicaea in Bythynia, who flourished in the second part of the second century, earned especial fame by compiling a catalogue of more than 1000 stars. Ptolemy in his Almagest made use of this catalogue. It is obviously this fact to which Kepler refers in this letter.

lations completely reach the exactness of observations by the senses. Until this was done it seemed impossible to describe the movements of Mars more accurately. The reason why the description of the movements of Mars was thought to be especially difficult, applies not only to Mars but to all planets, but the reason is more manifest with Mars. . . . Remain in good health, my highly distinguished teacher, and prove by a letter that you still love me. My regards to all my teachers. I will send to all of them a copy of my funeral speech [on Tycho Brahe], which also contains my poem.

THE IMPERIAL MATHEMATICUS
AT THE COURT IN PRAGUE

Emperor Rudolph II really granted Kepler the position and the considerable salary which Tycho had received and thus the great astronomer had reached—only a few years after his cruel expulsion from Graz—the zenith of his career in Prague. Even in these years he did not receive his salary with full regularity, but he could enjoy the feeling of comparative economic security and he made every use of this great advantage by an intense concentration on his work.

In these years in Prague he published a work on optics in its relation to astronomy (1604) which was later supplemented by his *Dioptrice* (1611) and its problems of observation through telescope. In 1605 he wrote on the eclipse of the sun of October 12, 1605. A work on chronology trying to demonstrate why the year 5 B.C. should be considered as the year of Christ's birth appeared in 1606 and in the same year a detailed treatise on "the new star in the foot of Serpentarius"—a new star which Kepler rightly, in contrast to Galileo, took for a fixed star, as he could not ascertain a measurable parallax. A report on a comet, later named after Halley but observed already in September and October 1607 by Kepler, was published by him in 1608, a treatise on *Mercurius in the Sun* in 1609, a discussion of Galileo's *Star Herald* in 1610 and in the same year a writing on astrology addressed to Philipp Feselius, physician of the Margrave of Baden; in 1611 the treatise on the satellites of Jupiter appeared. The principal work, however, which Kepler completed during these years in Prague—a work which is still considered as one of the classics of modern science and perhaps the most important among the basic works of astronomy— is his *New Astronomy or Physics of the Heavens explored on the Basis of the Law of Causality and developed in Analyses of the Movements of Mars based on Observations by Tycho Brahe* (1609). Here are to be found the first two of the three astronomical laws which made Kepler's name immortal.

But aside from the publication of these books, Kepler, in his extended correspondence, puts down a considerable number of new insights and stimulating observations.

The following selections from Kepler's letters in

these years can give only a dim impression of the richness and variegated nature of his thought at the height of his powers.

To David Fabricius, a theologian in
East-Friesland.

Prague, December 2, 1602

. . . Please take what I wrote you about astrology seriously. If I remember rightly I have shown by systematic reflections as well as by examples that I do not reject it entirely. If you achieve something in this field you will earn much greater honor than I will, as astrology is of so much more direct use to men. . . . But remember, the moment you cross the borderlines of acute reasoning and the powers of the human mind, the further you have advanced according to your own conviction, the more I grow suspicious of your rather great credulity. Yet, wait a minute! I was wrong. Please, don't box my ears. I am unarmed. And as you said you would not spare anyone, I must be cautious so that you don't consider me, too, as an enemy. . . .

The stars are moved by a certain power which is responsive to the geometrical conditions on the globé, capable of producing movement and of counting time. If you expect me to call a spade a spade, I cannot help but call this power the faculty of reasoning or mind. . . .

The blue color of the sky belongs neither to the sky nor to the eye. For if this were not so, then in either case we would necessarily see a blue color in the same way day and night, even if no light but black color of the infinite ocean of the air would offer itself to the eye. But the blue color appears only when that deep black is a mixture of white and black overlaid by a weak light after the eye has adapted itself to the strong light around us during the day.

To David Fabricius

Prague, July 4, 1603

. . . Dear Fabricius, your eagerness for truth deserves acknowledgment. However, one will not make any advance in this matter [the eccentricity of the earth-orbit] by conjectures of this type. We will never get any result if we do not presuppose something as certain and stable. You believe that I start with imagining some pleasant hypothesis and please myself in embellishing it, examining it only later by observations. In this you are very much mistaken. The truth is that after having built up a hypothesis on the ground of observations and given it proper foundations, I feel a peculiar desire to investigate whether I might discover some natural, pleasant combination between the two. But I never come to a final judgment in advance. One and a half years ago I spun some fantasies about cutting the eccentricity in half, but dropped these speculations because I always got the figure 2300 instead of 1800. The mistake had its origin in the observations which were not correctly reduced to the ecliptic; but I noticed this only much later. After correction of the mistake I at once received the number 1800 and received the same result in all experiments, of which I made not less than six, each time referring in some measure to six rotations. In this way I realized indeed this wonderful harmony in which observations and reasoning are evidently in accord in physics. . . .

To Edmund Bruce in Florence
　　　　　Prague, September 4, 1603
. . . Farewell! My greetings to Magini and Galileo, I am writing on the 4th of September

after having discovered Mercury in the early morning at a distance of 7°18′ from Venus, in a line leading from Mars through Venus. . . .

To Herwart

Prague, March 28, 1605

. . . You ask me, Magnificence, about the hypotheses of Copernicus and you seem to be pleased that I insist on my opinion. . . .

[One of my main ideas aimed against Tycho is] if the sun moves round the earth, then it must, of necessity, along with the other planets become sometimes faster, sometimes slower in its movements, and this without following fixed courses, since there are none. But this is incredible. Furthermore, the sun which is so much higher ranking than the unimportant earth would have to be moved by the earth in the same way as the five other planets are put in motion by the sun. That is completely absurd. Therefore it is much more plausible that the earth together with the five planets is put in motion by the sun and only the moon by the earth.

To Johann Georg Brengger, physician of the town
of Kaufbeuren

Prague, October 4, 1607

. . . Please, forgive me for not answering in detail, as I am extremely busy. I am just completing my investigation concerning the movements of the star Mars, and this demands a good deal of troublesome cogitation. I furnish a heavenly philosophy (or physics) in place of the heavenly theology or metaphysics of Aristotle. If you could only read my work and advise me before I publish it! It will be printed by Vögelin in Heidelberg. The circulation of single copies has been prohibited by the Emperor. Along with my physics I am at the same time teaching a new arithmetic. . . . Yet what am I driving at! It is not Mars who impelled me to write but something else. "There is a God in us; if he puts us in motion we are getting warmed up." Your letter is prophetic. You write how one has to measure the parallax of a comet. And behold, there appears a comet. I saw it for the first time on the 26th of September (others on the 25th of September). [In the following Kepler gives some information concerning the locus of the comet.] Be

content with this. You are a better observer than
I am.

To King James of England
With a copy of his book
A New Star in the Foot of Serpentarius

Prague, October, 1607

. . . Herewith I tender most respectfully to Your
Holy Majesty this my book by the kindness of His
Majesty's Ambassador present in this country.

May the good and almighty God ordain that
your Majesty rule so happily over Britain that you
never feel compelled to abandon philosophy because of excessive business. May the endeavors . . .
of your Majesty . . . to pacify . . . the Church
just reestablished under the most difficult circumstances be led by God to the blessing of Christianity.

[The dedication of the book presented to
the King runs as follows:]

"To the King-Philosopher the serving philosopher; to the Plato, the ruler of Britain, Diogenes
at Prague [14] asking Alexander for a gift sends . . .

[14] "Diogenes at Prague asking Alexander"—this is an allusion
by which Kepler in Prague compares himself with the Greek phil-

from his hired barrel this, his philosophical writing."

To Johann Georg Brengger

Heidelberg, November 30, 1607

. . . You think the nature of the starglobes quite pure and simple. I should think that they are similar to our earth. Being a philosopher you quote from a philosopher. If one would ask him he would refer to experience. But experience is silent, as no one ever visited the stars. Experience, therefore, says neither yes nor no. I refer in my probable inference to the similarity of the moon to the earth. On the moon much is similar to the terrestrial conditions. In my opinion there is also humidity on the stars . . . and therefore living creatures who benefit from these conditions. Not only the unfortunate Bruno [15] who was burned in Rome on red-hot coals,

---

osopher Diogenes of Sinope, one of the leaders of the Greek Cynics in the 4th century B.C. According to a famous anecdote Diogenes of Sinope did not live in a house but in a hired barrel. When Alexander, the Great King of Macedonia, offered him to fulfil any wish he would utter, Diogenes is said to have answered from his barrel: "Please get out of the sun in front of my barrel!"

[15] Giordano Bruno (1548–1600), the well known Italian thinker and poet whose importance as a philosopher and scientist has

but also the venerated Brahe was of the opinion
that there are living creatures on the stars. I, too,
am a follower of this opinion especially as I maintain with Aristarchus, that the earth has motion
in common with the planets. . . .

To Johann Georg Brengger

Prague, April 5, 1608
. . . I heard from Mr. Wackher [16] that Bruno
has been burnt in Rome; he is said to have been un-
yielding during the execution. He maintained the
futility of all forms of religion and transformed
the divine being into the world, into circles and
points. . . .

My opinion that there are unseen comets in the
sky is disputed by many. One asks how I could
know this. But I do not say that I do know it, I
only think it probable. You believe that one should
see them, if they exist. I deny this. For, if they follow their course far away from the earth, it is quite

often been greatly overestimated, was imprisoned by the Inquisi-
tion from 1592–1600 and on February 17, 1600, burned on the
Campofiore in Rome on account of heresy.

[16] Johann Matthias Wackher von Wackhenfels, councilor at
the court in Prague, with whom Kepler entertained friendly relations even years after he had left the Bohemian Capital.

possible, if they are small, that one does not see them. What does Aristotle say? Does he not say that many pass in the daytime which one cannot see because of daylight? Who told this to Aristotle? I did not say and also do not believe that the matter of the comets has been created out of nothing. To create means to create from matter even if this already existed. It is not absurd either to assume that the starglobes evaporate into the ether. How, if the earth also evaporates into the ether? Whither, do you think, escapes the matter which is left after the burning of meteors? Do you not daily see how large pieces of wood burn? Weigh the ashes accurately and conclude therefrom how much matter escapes upwards. . . .

You prophesied rightly that the theologians would be offended. They have prohibited indeed the printing of the book in Leipzig, because of the last sentence about the creation of the spirit. I have therefore changed the straightforward expression in the Latin text. Yet I do not believe that my opinion is so absurd. . . . I believe that the spirit is not created out of nothing, but of heavenly matter, and afterwards it is illuminated and instructed by a ray out of God's image. . . .

JOHANNES KEPLER:

On the difference between a "geometrical
kabbala" [17] and exact physics

To Joachim Tanckius, Professor of Anatomy
and Surgery in Leipzig

Prague, May 12, 1608

. . . I too play with symbols; I have started a
small work *Geometrical Kabbala*; it deals with the
"ideas" of the things of nature in geometry. And
yet, all the time I am playing I never forget that
I am playing. For we can never prove anything
with symbols; in the philosophy of nature no hidden things can be revealed by geometrical symbols,
but only things already known can be put together. . . .

To David Fabricius

Prague, November 10, 1608

. . . I do not know what to say to your conclu-
sions concerning the theory of Mars, which you recommended to me with the gesture of a Pythagoras

[17] Kabbalah (meaning literally "tradition") is the name which
Jewish mystics used for the characterization of their speculations
from post-biblical times throughout the centuries. In the Kabbalah the mystical interpretation of figures and geometrical symbols has often played a considerable part.

and invite me to admire. Shall I laugh? But you deserve something better by virtue of your extraordinary industry and your unimpeachable conduct. . . . You say that geometry bore you a daughter. I looked at her, she is beautiful, but she will become a very bad wench who will seduce all the men of the many daughters which mother physics has borne me. Your theory will attract lecturers and philosophers; it will offer a way out to the enemies of the physics of the sky, the patrons of ignorance . . . in this way they can escape the fetters of my physical demonstrations and gain a liberty in which they can form their own gods. . . . Yes, I will do my best for our science, but not in recommending a wrong doctrine or in striving for popularity. If one is expected to bring forth only that which pleases the masses, why do we lecture at all on astronomy, why on geometry, sciences which are entirely beyond the understanding of the masses, and receive, therefore, little appreciation? Yes, this I will do: I will interweave Copernicus into the revised astronomy and physics, so that either both sciences will perish or both will keep alive. But, if one may prophesy, I believe that the whole rubbish of polemic books along with their writers and their peevish brains will perish before Aristarchus [18] and Copernicus will be given up.

At what a high price, however, Kepler had acquired this assurance of his basic astronomical tenets, is well described in a letter of 1605, speaking of his extended studies in the movements of the planet Mars: "I ran against thousands of walls until I, finally, was pushed into this one [right] direction."

On Galileo's work *Sidereus Nuncius* (1610)

. . . After my opinion on Galileo's *Sidereus Nuncius* had already been printed, some of my friends observed that they felt it was somehow too unrestrained. One wished I had cut out the introduction. Another wanted some phrases mitigated which might in easy-going people arouse the impression that I attributed to an adversary ideas which differ from the common opinion of the schools. Everybody wished that I had been more economical in my praise toward Galileo so that

[18] Aristarchus of Samos (about 300 B.C.) has sometimes been called "the Copernicus of Antiquity." He—and in greater detail Seleukus of Seleukia about 150 B.C.—developed the hypothesis of the movement of the earth whereupon Aristarchus was already called "blasphemer" by the Stoic Cleanthes.

there should be room left for the opinions of quite important men who, as one learns, dissent from my views.

I have therefore wished to remind the reader that everyone likes his own way best, that most people get heated in their discussions and that, in my opinion, humor is by far the best seasoning of any debate. Others, in philosophizing, try to impress people with too much grave solemnity but very often give a ridiculous impression this way quite against their will. I believe that I am made for mitigating the troubles and bothers of research work by expressing good humor in my style.

. . . I have always stuck to the habit of praising what, according to my opinion, others have done well and of rejecting what they have done badly. Never am I a despiser or concealer of another man's knowledge if my own is failing. I never feel submissive to others or forget myself, if out of my own capacity I have done things better or discovered them sooner. Nor do I believe that the Italian Galileo has earned so much of my gratitude, that I, the German, should flatter him for it, by adjusting truth and my deepest conviction to him.

None, however, should believe that by my frank

agreement with Galileo others should be deprived
of the liberty to differ from us. I praised him without prejudice to any other person's judgment. I
have also undertaken here to defend some of my
own statements. But although I have done this in
all sincerity believing in their truth, I promise that
I will discard them without hesitation if anyone
more learned than I will correctly prove to me why
I am mistaken.

To Galileo in Padua

Prague, August 9, 1610

I have received your observations on the Medi-
cean stars from the Ambassador of his Highness
the Grand Duke of Tuscany. You have aroused in
me a passionate desire to see your instruments, so
that I at last, like you, might enjoy the great per-
formance in the sky. Of the oculars which we have
here the best has a tenfold enlargement, the others
hardly a threefold; the only one which I have
gives a twentyfold enlargement, but the light is very
weak. The reason for this is not unknown to me and
I see how the intensity could be improved, but one
hesitates to spend the money.

. . . In my opinion, no one is entitled to charge a person with having taken over another's ideas unless he is able to recognize and . . . understand the new, rare, and beautifully original ideas which the other has pronounced. To me it is an insult . . . if someone wants to praise me because of my reputation in order to slander others. Nothing annoys me more than the praise of such a man; what an outcast of a human being! He fantastically ascribes to me doubts about the value of your discoveries, because I allow everyone his own opinion. What lack of judgment! The considerations of others need not necessarily be in accord with my own. Regarding something as true, I am, nevertheless, able to tolerate others who are not of the same opinion.

. . . O, you wise Pythagoras, who believed that the majesty of philosophy is present in nothing but silence! But now the die is cast. You, my Galileo, have opened the holy of the holiest of the skies. What else can you do but despise the noise which has been created. . . . The crowd takes vengeance on itself by remaining in eternal ignorance in consequence of its contempt for philosophy. . . .

JOHANNES KEPLER:

Galileo's answer to Kepler

Padua, August 19, 1610

. . . What is to be done now? Shall we follow Democritus or Heraclitus? [19] We will laugh at the extraordinary stupidity of the crowd, my Kepler. What do you say to the main philosophers of our school, who, with the stubbornness of vipers, never wanted to see the planets, the moon or the telescope although I offered them a thousand times to show them the planets and the moon. Really, as some have shut their ears, these have shut their eyes towards the light of truth. This is an awful thing, but it does not astonish me. This sort of person thinks that philosophy is a book like the Aeneid or Odyssey and that one has not to search for truth in the world of nature, but in the comparisons of texts (to use their own words).

Why have I no time to laugh a little longer with you! How you would burst out laughing, my dear Kepler, if you would hear what the greatest phi-

[19] According to Seneca, *De ira*, lib. II, cap. 10 and Lucian, *Vitarum auctio*, chap. 13 ed. by Julius Sommerbrodt, 1889, vol. I, 2, p. 28, Democritus was said to be the laughing philosopher and Heraclitus the weeping one.

losopher of the "Gymnasium" told the Grand Duke
about me when, with logical reasons as if they were
magic formulas, he wanted to tear the planets from
the heavens and dispute them away till nothing was
left of them! But night begins, I cannot continue
to chat with you. Farewell, highly learned gentleman, and continue to show your good-will toward
me.

After the death of Tycho, Kepler certainly held
a position of undeniable social distinction in Prague,
and he was granted a very good salary on paper.
But these were tumultuous times, and the payment
of the salary was irregular. Even more important,
however, for a man of Kepler's sensitivity, was the
fact that his real achievements were hardly recognized by anyone in Prague during the years of his
outwardly greatest successes: and his prestige was
essentially based on the type of work which he per-
formed in compliance with demands and interests
alien to him. Jean Baptiste Delambre observed in
his *Histoire de l'astronomie moderne* that none of
the astronomers who were Kepler's contemporaries,
including Galileo, conferred any adequate praise

on the discovery of the three laws [20] which, since
Newton and the promulgation of the theory of
gravity, have immortalized the name of Kepler.
From this one may infer how much less Emperor
Rudolph II and the court of Prague were impressed
by the painstaking labor which Kepler devoted to
laying the foundations of modern astronomy as an
exact theoretical science. They were interested in
useful prophecies of political events and of personal
human fate derived from the constellation of the
stars, and they often grew impatient when they felt
how much more emphasis Kepler placed on practically valueless "speculations."

In about the same years the theosophist Jacob
Böhme attracted the attention of the Elector and
the Court at Dresden for a short time. But when the
Dresden Court discovered that Böhme's use of
alchemic terms had only a symbolic, religious
meaning, and would never lead to any production

[20] The three laws are:
  1) The planets describe ellipses with the sun at the focus of
     each ellipse.
  2) A line drawn from a planet to the sun sweeps over equal
     areas in equal times.
  3) The squares of the periodic times are proportional to the
     cubes of the mean distances from the sun.

of gold by alchemic manipulations, they lost all interest in him; they let him feel their disappointment even far more brutally than this was ever the case with Kepler in Prague. But Kepler, too, even during his stay in Prague, had ample evidence of the total misjudgment of his true scientific aims and achievements. Often he succeeded only with difficulty in warding off his critics by using every ounce of his diplomatic skill, his genuine benevolence, patience and good humor.

In a letter to Petrus Wok Orsini at the beginning of 1602, he writes, for instance, that, like a psychiatrist who wants to prescribe some medicine to a madman, he had often to "adapt himself in words and gestures to the confused talk of the mentally diseased"; and in other cases, he could meet unfair ridicule of his work only by turning the "blind back of my head" toward his opponents. As late as in 1609 he writes to Emperor Rudolph, in the dedication of his *Astronomia Nova,* that "one must just tolerate certain rude jokes of the type that is common among soldiers," if one has adversaries and deals with such a "warlike" topic as the planet Mars, the star of the God of War.

In September 1603, when Kepler complained to

Herwart that he had not received any salary for the current year, he still thought of resigning from his position in Prague and of going to Swabia. In 1604 in his dedication of *Astronomiae Pars Optica* he also reminds the Emperor that he needs further financial support.

Parts from the dedication-letter to the *Astronomiae Pars Optica*

. . . If your Majesty would graciously agree with my most humble intentions, I would feel really happy; even more so, if you would find something in this work which satisfies your excellent judgment in all sciences; . . . but I would feel most happy, if the kindness which I have experienced so far would not be withdrawn from me. Then I would not have to fear that the most fatal enemy of science, sorrow, after having knocked me down by hunger, would expel me from this my office, the fortress confided to my sense of duty. Then I shall never doubt that your Majesty will send me, in time, those subsidies by means of which I can stand this siege, and after having conquered all difficulties in the end may happily finish my other work to God's honor, in praise of your Majesty and for the benefit of mankind. . . .

In November 1604, in a letter to the Elector Maximilian of Bavaria, Kepler also mentions that he receives an honorable salary from the Emperor only as far as the "enormous war expenses permit payment" of this salary. To his old teacher Mästlin who praised him because he did not look down on him in his elevated position at the Emperor's Court, Kepler gives a description of his life in Prague which has a particularly true ring in its modesty, self-irony and inner awareness of his true vocation. "I am living here," so he writes to Mästlin on March 5, 1605, "on the stage of the world as a single private person, glad if I can squeeze out part of my salary from the Court. Besides I fancy myself and conduct myself as if I did not serve the Emperor but the whole of mankind and posterity. Confident of this I despise, with secret pride, all the honors and distinctions of the world, and if necessary also those who bestow these honors. The only honor I recognize as such is that bestowed by providence which has allowed me to make use of Tycho's observations."

Even during the years in Prague, Kepler could devote only half of his time to his proper studies, the other half, as he writes to Longomontanus in 1605, belongs to the work for the Court, to which he had to make a daily trip of about an hour; and in the same year he also reports, in a letter to Caspar Odontius, an assistant of his, that he was bound to give a detailed account of the use of his time to the Father Confessor and a Counselor of the Emperor named Johannes Pistorius in such a way that he could not engage in any private and public research work without the knowledge of his Imperial sponsor. He relates, in a letter to Herwart on January 13, 1606, that he had, of course, to be frequently at the disposal of his patron and his princely friends for extraordinary services.

Nevertheless, won over by the nobility, the integrity and charm of Kepler's character, Pistorius as well as the Emperor obviously showed genuine benevolence toward their "Imperial mathematician." Pistorius, in a letter of July 12, 1607 harshly rejects all the theological views of Kepler, but he praises his mathematical genius and assures him of his "affection so well deserved."

To live in one of the centers of the political life

of his time and to be associated with some of the mighty of the earth, held in itself little or no attraction to Kepler. As he writes to Brengger, on November 30, 1607, he wished by no means for his stepdaughter to marry any of those ambitious young men who listen to the "song of sirens" at the Imperial Court. Throughout his life, Kepler contacted many princes and noblemen, sent them his books and wrote dedicatory letters to them which may sound today rather subservient, but were remarkably restrained in tone compared with most of similar documents of those times. Yet Kepler evidently never had any interest in social or political prestige in itself. On the contrary, he was afraid of being distracted by it. All he wished to receive from sovereigns and other high personalities of political or financial influence was the means to concentrate fully on his research work.

How irritable he sometimes was when he had to encounter even minor disturbances in the midst of his absorbing studies, may be inferred, for instance, from the following, half serious, half humorous letter which he wrote on December 10, 1604, to his friend and specially faithful patron Herwart.

JOHANNES KEPLER:

To Johann Georg Herwart

Prague, December 10, 1604
I am writing to Your Magnificence, quite disturbed on account of the difficult circumstances in which I find myself. . . .

Only quite recently I received copies of my book and therefore have not yet had the chance to start with the corrections. Except in some few copies the title and dedication are missing. They have been omitted through lack of supervision in Frankfurt. Pressing domestic troubles have been preventing me from supervising the bookbinder with the necessary care . . .

The domestic disturbance, which has produced this confusion (I must mention it in order to be fully excused) is caused by the women. What trouble, what fuss and what disturbance is created by inviting fifteen to sixteen women to my wife in childbed, to be hospitable and to see them to the door etc. You must understand, that on the 3rd of December a son was born to me and baptized the day before yesterday . . .

One of the major difficulties to Kepler's undisturbed pursuit of his astronomical investigations arose, in the earlier years in Prague, from the attitude of Tycho's heirs. On October 1, 1602, in a letter to David Fabricius, Kepler describes the beginning of these differences with high impartiality: "The root of the controversies lies in the bad habits and the suspicion of the family but also in my own passion and the pleasure I take in teasing others. Thus Tengnagel [the son-in-law of Tycho Brahe] found no small reason for suspecting me of bad designs. I had in my possession Tycho's observations and refused to return them to his heirs. Yet Franz [Tengnagel] was never satisfied with any of my offers to come to an agreement with him by compromise; but he . . . suddenly turned against me with threats . . . as if I were a low slave." The further development of the relationship with Tycho's heirs may be inferred again from a letter to Fabricius to whom Kepler reports on Febr. 7, 1604.

To David Fabricius

Prague, February 7, 1604
. . . I cannot give you any exact information about the state of affairs among the Tychonians,

because Tengnagel keeps me away. He is like a dog in the manger, who does not eat any hay himself but does not let anyone else approach either. He receives 1000 gulden every year. Now he wishes to assure his income by my research. On condition that he gives me the fourth part of his thousand, I agreed to put my own work at his disposal and to assume responsibility before the Emperor on behalf of both of us. But as he wants to enjoy the thousand gulden all by himself I . . . am obliged to ask for a salary for myself. I did the same when I presented the *Optics*, the *Mars-ephemerides* and the revised edition of *Moontables* on January the 1st. When Tengnagel saw this, he pretended that I upset the decisions made by Tycho and declared he did not want to provide me with observations. But the real reason is that he wants to put obstacles in my way in order to find time to work out something for himself. He maintains that he hopes to achieve something himself; however he is very unstable, dropping a word now and then that all this is not in his line. I swear solemnly that I won't undertake anything against him or his salary. But I passionately wish to acquire these observations which I desire, and to defend myself by exact statements and ex-

planations of the true facts, against any accusations
bruited about . . .

Tengnagel was a politically and scientifically
ambitious man, without having anything of the
genius of Kepler. But one of the comprehensible,
impersonal reasons for his frequent opposition to
Kepler was, of course, his fear of seeing Tycho's
life work distorted by Kepler's endeavors to put
this work into the service of the "untenable"
Copernican hypotheses and speculations which
Tycho had rejected.

The agreement which was finally reached in all
these controversies with Tycho Brahe's heirs was a
really ingenious diplomatic way out of these difficulties—an agreement, in all probability, suggested
by Kepler. Kepler generously allowed the ambitious
Tengnagel to write the following introductory note
to Kepler's *Astronomia Nova:*

Greetings to the Reader! I had the intention to
turn to you, reader, with a lengthier address. But
the multitude of political activities which keeps
me busy these days even more than usual and the
imminent departure of our Kepler . . . to Frank-

furt [to accelerate the print and publication of his *Astronomia Nova* in Western Germany] have given me only a moment of time for writing. I, therefore, thought I should address at least a few words to you so that you will not be confused by the liberty with which Kepler deviates from Brahe, especially in certain physical explanations. This liberty does not harm [the importance] of the *Rudolphine Tables* [whose preparation Brahe inaugurated by his observations]. Such liberty is to be found with all the philosophers from the day of creation. You will learn from the work itself that it is based on the foundations laid by Brahe, i.e., on his improved expositions about the fixed stars and the sun; and all the material (I mean the observations) are compiled by Brahe. Take, therefore, Kepler's present excellent work as a predecessor of the *Tables* and the *Observations* which in the present tumultuous times . . . can be published only after some delay . . .

The confidence which Emperor Rudolph placed in Kepler seems to have grown the longer he was in his service; and Kepler, with great tactfulness and understanding, advised the melancholy and half-insane sovereign as a psychologist rather than as an astrologist, as one may infer for instance from the following letter written to a confidant of the Emperor:

Prague, Easter 1611

. . . Ordinary astrology is a cothurnus and can easily be used to please both parties [in political controversies]. I believe that in such weighty reflections one should not only exclude ordinary astrology but also the one which I have recognized as being in accord with nature. I certainly do not give you this warning because you might need it at solemn conferences; I know one does not discuss such things on these occasions. But this little fox [astrological superstition] waylays you only the more secretely at home, in the bedroom, on the couch, deep down in the soul and sometimes provides you with ideas which, tempted by him, one brings forth at public meetings without perceiving from where the ideas came. . . .

In short, I am of the opinion that astrology has to be withdrawn not only from the Senate but also from the heads of those who want to advise the

Emperor today to the best of their abilities; one must keep astrology entirely from the Emperor's mind.

In his later years, Rudolph withdrew from political life and his more aggressive brother Matthias forced him to give up the reign over more and more territory of his empire. Rudolph finally could not even pay his soldiers. Riots broke out in Prague and everywhere in Germany unrest and conflicts made themselves felt, the forerunners of the Thirty Years' War. Under these circumstances, Kepler had to intensify his endeavors to find a new position outside Prague. As always, he would have liked best a professorship at his old university Tübingen in his native Württemberg. Again, his homesickness breaks eloquently through in those last years of his stay at the Imperial Court; and after he had failed in all his numerous attempts to receive a permanent appointment from one of the other European princes, he succeeded in winning over the Duke of Württemberg.

In 1611, the Duke and his political advisers were willing to grant a permanent professorship to the son of their country who had meanwhile risen to considerable fame at the Court in Prague. But the Protestant theologians of Württemberg protested against his appointment. Kepler had frankly confessed his liberal religious views in a letter to the Duke; and in an official testimony of April 25, 1611, the members of the Württemberg consistory declared that those ultra-liberal views of Kepler on the Lord's Supper made it impossible for them to consider him as their "brother in Christ." They stamped Kepler as a sly and untrustworthy Calvinist, who should be at all costs prevented from poisoning the minds of Swabian youth by his heterodox beliefs. This document of the theologians made Kepler's appointment in Tübingen impossible.

But in the same year, he was hit by an even much harder blow of fate, the death of his wife and one of his sons. How deeply the experience of their suffering during their illness cut into the soul of the tender, perceptive man, we learn from a letter which he wrote many months after his loss. This letter could hardly be more moving if it had come from the pen of a great poet.

JOHANNES KEPLER:

On the Death of his Wife
To Tobias Scultetus, Councilor at the Court of the Emperor Matthias, and friend of Kepler

Prague, April 13, 1612

. . . Apart from the public misfortunes and the threats from outside, disaster in my own home has come over me in many ways. . . . I had a life companion, I do not want to call her my dearest one, for that is always or should always be the case; no, a woman to whom public opinion offered the palm of respectability, righteousness and modesty. In a rare way she combined these virtues with outward beauty and cheerfulness of mind. Not to mention her inward virtues, her piety towards God and charity towards the poor. With her I had blossoming children, especially a six-year-old boy, very much like his mother. . . . In every way one could call him a morning hyacinth of the first springdays whose delicate scent filled the room with an ambrosiac aroma. The boy was so tenderly united with his mother that one could not say that both were "weak with love" for each other, but rather mad with such love. I had to witness how, in her prime, my wife for three whole years was continuously afflicted with attacks of the raging tumors in her body, how she was shaken and in the end so shattered that she not seldom was mentally deranged and quite out of her mind. And just when she seemed to be recovering she was thrown back into a depression over one illness after another of her beloved children and was wounded to the depths of her heart by the death of the little boy who was half her heart to her. Paralyzed by the atrocious deeds of the soldiers, and eyewitness of the battle in the town; driven to despair for a better future and out of the inextinguishable longing for her lost darling in the end she caught the Hungarian fever (her charity took revenge on her, as she would not stop looking after the sick). In a melancholic depression, the saddest mental condition under the sun, she at last breathed out her soul. The sympathy of the people was so great, that some exclaimed at the funeral, now she had gone there was no good woman left on earth. . . . Obviously I should be reminded of how much better the mild shepherd of the soul has cared for her. . . .

Why do I speak of all this? Am I the only one who is treated cruelly by fate? Well, please learn from my report about my state of mind, since to their astonishment some think I no longer show that elasticity which speculations in astronomy demand.

Kepler stayed in Prague until after the death of Emperor Rudolph II in 1612. After Rudolph's successor, Matthias, had confirmed his rank as "Imperial Mathematicus," but had given him permission to accept another position outside the Court, he left Prague for Linz while he had to leave his two children in the care of relatives in a little town named Wels in Upper Austria.

THE DIFFICULT YEARS IN LINZ

In Linz, as once in Graz, Kepler held a teaching position at a kind of college, the *"Landschafts- schule"* and in addition to his classes on mathematics he was put in charge of drawing new maps of Upper Austria. With some interruptions, he lived in this Austrian city on the Danube, not far from the Bavarian frontier, from 1612 to the end of 1626. But these fifteen years were certainly not happier than his life in Prague. Soon after his arrival in Linz, he was excluded from participation in the Holy Communion in Linz. The "Minister Primarius" of Linz, Daniel Hitzler, was a schoolmate of Kepler in Tübingen, and he obviously remembered from the days of his youth what a "dangerous" religious liberal the astronomer was. Apart from this, as we saw, Kepler had always frankly confessed his reluctance to subscribe blindly to the doctrine of the ultra-orthodox Protestant Church of Württemberg. Therefore, Hitzler, in his capacity of the highest ranking minister in Linz, did not admit the astronomer to the Holy Communion. One can hardly gauge today what this exclusion from Communion meant to Kepler, whose social reputation and good standing was in this way noticeably impaired. Small wonder, therefore, that Kepler protested in a letter to the Württemberg consistory against Hitzler's procedure. But in a detailed reply to Kepler's protest and self-defense, the highest organ of the Protestant Church in Swabia definitely sided with the pastor in Linz against the Linz astronomer of international fame. Kepler, however, remained upright in his religious convictions, and one will notice only a much subdued excitement over these controversies when he indicates his own enlightened and tolerant views in a letter to Mästlin:

To Michael Mästlin

Linz, December 22, 1616
. . . In these quarrelsome times, when mankind is splitting into so many different parties, the feeling of belonging together gives one some consolation. Therefore, please take notice that I side with the Confession of Augsburg and with the work of Chemnitz which stands against the Council of Trent.[21] I am not in favor of any teaching which

21 Martin Chemnitz (1522–1586) was one of the most influential Lutheran theologians of the sixteenth century. His 4 volume

cannot be found in the old Fathers of the Church or is undisputed by the present parties. Whoever is accusing me of the slightest passion for innovation is not fair to me . . . I could put an end to the whole quarrel if I subscribed to the formulas of the concordate. Yet it is not my way to become a hypocrite in matters of conscience. I am willing to subscribe only if one takes into account my reservations already mentioned. I will not take part in the fury of the theologians. I will not stand as a judge over my brethren; for whether they stand or fall, they are brethren of mine in the Lord. As I am not a teacher of the Church, it will suit me better to pardon others and think well of them rather than accuse and misinterpret them.

In 1619, however, in a letter to his former theology teacher, Hafenreffer, some comprehensibly stronger indignation flares up when he looks back

---

work *Examen Concilii Tridentini* (1565–1573) has been the arsenal of Protestant arguments against Catholicism up to the nineteenth century. Kepler joins Chemnitz in believing that the decrees of the Catholic Church at the Council of Trent cannot claim to be based on the authority of the Bible or the Church Fathers.

at the seven years of his exclusion from Communion. When in Tübingen, Kepler had asked Hafenreffer for mediation with the theological authorities in his affair. But Kepler never heard that the timid and orthodox Hafenreffer intervened on his behalf. With almost too great a humility toward his teacher, but at the same time with general vigor and firmness, he answers the conventional theological admonitions of Hafenreffer as follows:

To Matthias Hafenreffer, Professor
of Theology in Tübingen

Linz, April 11, 1619

I have received your letter. Modesty and veneration fought with each other as to whether or not to answer it. Modesty demanded indulgence for the outstanding man, and indulgence towards my reputation to avoid the impression of being garrulous. Veneration demanded excuse for what had been understood differently from the way in which I had meant it. The shyness of modesty was conquered by the pain which would originate from the veneration, if I left my great benefactor under

the misapprehension of my words and actions; for
to be condemned by him would mean doom. I
entreat you, let a bright, friendly face shine on
this letter so that my wounded heart, warmed
and strengthened by it, may quiet down somehow . . .

. . . You praised my knowledge of astronomy in
order to dispute my theological views in the same
breath. . . . "Why does he not want to subscribe?
Surely because he is looking for astronomical
sophistry in theology." Beware, that you do not
punish an innocent person with exclusion. It is not
sophistry but brotherly love if I do not want to condemn those who want to adhere to the old teachings
but would follow them rather than the Formula of
Concord, in the article about Christ as a person. I
know that your adversaries have sinned against
love; but that is not my concern. I know that we
have to be good to our enemy and to love those who
hate us, that is, that we should examine their dic-
tum regardless of their having sinned against love.
If you theologians cannot follow me there as a
layman, I will not, therefore, stubbornly reject
your officialdom. If I said something audacious, I

am willing to withdraw according to your demand, and be silent about it. . . .

If it hurts you to read the gloomy prophecies about the Church, so, indeed, it hurts me to write them. But the bitterness is so great in both quarreling parties that it is decidedly to be regarded as a very bad omen. . . . In Styria the beginning of all evil certainly started in an especially sharp tone delivered from the pulpit by Fischer and Kelling. Fischer at times displayed his cloak at the pulpit and asked whether it were decent if the women were hidden under his cloak; it would be much more indecent, he said, if one painted monks under the cloak of the Virgin Mary. Therefore, I believe, that being looked on as a prophet . . . I fulfill my vocation best in prophesying that evil will arise from such behavior, which could be avoided by correcting it. If you have understood these my good intentions, you will no longer be angry with me because of my prophecies . . .

My exclusion has now lasted for seven full years. The servants of the Church in this town always affirm they would be willing to admit me if I could receive admission from the council or theological faculty of Württemberg. But up to now I have never received a categorical decision from the theologians, which would give me to understand whether or not I were ultimately excluded. Therefore after long waiting I repeat my request for an answer; I must not let matters drift to a point where I become a permanent living offense.

Even this letter, however, was of no avail. Kepler remained excluded from Communion in Linz. Later, however, in 1620, when Hitzler was removed from his post in Linz during the siege of the city by the Duke of Bavaria, Kepler showed the man who had excluded him from Christian Communion what real Christian brotherhood is and in the genuine superiority of his mind and heart showed no longer any grudge against Hitzler's former unchristian aggressiveness.

When Kepler, the widower, came to settle in Linz in 1612, busy tongues were ready to spread the rumor that by his unorthodox half Calvinist and half "Popish" views, by his stargazing and insufficient income, he had driven his wife insane. In a lengthy letter to a lady whose name remained anonymous, Kepler took much pains to demonstrate that stargazing is not a dishonorable profession, and no fair lady should be ashamed to be called *"Frau Sternseherin."* In earlier times, he interestingly observes, when there were only a few scholars, all of them were derogatorily called "students"; and since there are now so few astronomers, they also are looked down on. Later when their number had increased they, too, like the doctors and theologians, would be far more respected. Real noblemen, emperors, kings and princes, as he adds, even now show far more esteem for stargazers than middle-class people in provincial towns.

Above all, however, Kepler gives in this letter a detailed picture of his domestic life, which reveals a rare frankness, honesty and tenderness of heart. His honesty admits that sometimes he may not have shown enough understanding and patience toward the increasingly melancholy moods of his wife. Especially when he was immersed in "severe studies," and she pestered him with too many household affairs, he may have answered her too briefly and abruptly, and finally not have answered at all. But he had never called her a fool, although she may have inferred something like that in her oversensitiveness. He relates that his late wife had read a good deal but never his scholarly theological disquisitions. He never imposed on her his liberal religious views in which he indeed disapproved of the common Lutheran suspicion toward Catholics and all non-Lutherans. It must have been either the "devil," or some of those inquisitive wives of intolerant Lutheran clergymen who spread the rumor that his "high flown" religious views had detrimentally influenced the mental health of his wife. And he further reports that sometimes she had indeed been irritable and even rude toward her servants, and had resented any dispraising word on his part, even when she had acted high-handedly. But he assures his correspondent, with a stirring sincerity, that whenever he saw that his wife took any of his words to heart he would have "rather bitten his finger" than hurt her with any further reproach; and it "never came to a hostility between us, as we both knew too well how deeply our hearts remained attached to each other."

Yet thinking of his motherless children and of himself, Kepler did not wish to be unmarried for a long time; and so toward the end of 1613, he found another life-companion, Susanne Reuttinger, a girl of twenty-four years, who, eighteen years his junior, had been educated in the house of the Baroness Starhemberg in Efferdingen. In a letter to the Baron Strahlendorf in Prague on October 23, he announces his forthcoming re-marriage and describes with special humor how difficult it was for him to make his final choice between "eleven candidates" in question, although he received much advice from many friends.

To Baron Peter Heinrich von Strahlendorf in Prague

Efferdingen near Linz, October 23, 1613

Though all Christians begin their wedding invitation by declaring solemnly that they are entering into married life owing to a special divine management, I, as a philosopher, would like to talk in greater detail about this with you, the great wise man. . . . Was it divine providence or moral guilt on my part which has torn my mind in the last two years and longer into so many different directions and which let me listen to so many people . . . so divergent from each other? Was it divine management that brought in all these various persons and their actions? There is nothing I want to find out and long to know with greater urgency than this: can I find God, whom I can almost grasp with my own hands in looking at the universe, also in myself? . . . As I believe, nothing extraordinary has happened to me. I believe that everyone of us has experience similar to mine, not only once but very often. The difference is only that the others do not worry about it, as I do, that they forget more easily and get over it more quickly than I do, or that they have more self-control and settle their unhappiness by themselves. . . . I had been fighting long and heavily with this sorrow, waiting for the visit of the wife of Herrn Helmhard wondering if she would recommend to me the third [recommended candidate] and this would decide in favor of the third instead of the last two. After having heard the woman at last I decided on the fourth, annoyed at having to let the fifth slip away. Just when I was going to settle the matter . . . fate took over: the fourth had grown tired of my hesitations and given her word to another who for a long time had emphatically asked for her hand and reassured her with promises. I was now as much annoyed about the loss of the fourth as I had been about losing the fifth. . . . There is something wrong with my feelings; I stirred them up anew every day by my hesitation, comparing and weighing the reasons pro and con. And yet it proved to be no misfortune for me that I had no success with the fourth, for evidently this was best for both parties. As far as the fifth is concerned there is still the question of why, though she was destined for me, God permitted that she had six rivals in the course of one year? Could my uneasy heart not learn to be content with its fate only by realizing the impossibility of the fulfillment of all its other desires?

. . . This is the commentary on the words with which I began my invitation. You see how providence drove me into these needs in order to learn that high rank, wealth and parentage, of which my bride has none, must be ignored and the other simpler virtues be sought for. Her name is SUSANNA; her parents were Johann Reuttinger and Barbara, citizens of Efferdingen. The father was a carpenter by profession. Both parents have already died. She received her education, which must take the place of a dowry, at the home of the Starhembergs. . . . No unnecessary pride, no unnecessary pomp, industry and some knowledge of taking over a household, middle-aged and a brain capable of learning what is still lacking. I shall be married to this person according to the arrangement of the Squire of Starhemberg on the coming October 30th at 12 o'clock. The wedding meal will be served in the Golden Lion. . . . Farewell and let me know through your secretary if I can expect you, so that the innkeeper can be informed.

To Matthias Bernegger, Professor of
History in Strassburg

Regensburg, October 18, 1613
(announcing the day of his second wedding)
. . . The wedding will take place on the day of the eclipse of the moon when the astronomical spirit is in hiding, as I want to rejoice in the festival day. . . .

Kepler's second wife bore him seven children, two of whom died at an early age. Yet, during the rest of his life, he took care not only of the surviving five and the two from his first marriage, but also the two children of his ne'er-do-well brother Heinrich.

Again, the years in Linz as those in Graz and

Prague saw the completion of a considerable number of writings by Kepler. There are several treatises on problems of chronological character: the *Dialogus de Calendario Gregoriano,* published more than a century later in 1726; a German version of the work of 1606 on the year of Christ's birth, printed in 1613; and in the same year, a memorandum recommending the introduction of the Gregorian calendar despite objections of Protestant theologians against this "Popish innovation." This memorandum was written for the *Reichstag* in Regensburg at the request of the Emperor; but Kepler's recommendations were generally accepted only about a hundred years later. Also *Ad espistolam Sethi Calvisii Chronologi Responsio* [22] [1614], a refutation of Calvisius' criticism of Kepler's views, and another writing on the year of Christ's birth *De vero anno quo Aeternus Dei Filius humanam naturam . . . assumpsit* (1614) [On the year in which the eternal son of God took on human nature] as well as the *Eclogae*

[22] This treatise is to be found in Christian Frisch, Joannis Kepleri Opera Omnia, 8 vols. Frankfurt und Erlangen, Hayder und Zimmer, 1858 ff., vol. IV, p. 271 ff.

Chronicae (1615) deal to a large extent with chronological questions. Very important stereogeo- metrical problems are discussed, and even some ap- proach to the problem of differential calculus is found in his *Nova stereometria doliorum vina- riorum* (New Stereometry of Wine Barrels) which also appeared in 1615. The occasion for writing this extremely valuable treatise, however, was noth- ing but the dissatisfaction which the thorough mind of Kepler felt when he saw the superficial manner in which sellers and buyers generally esti- mated the quantities of wine contained in barrels of various shapes. No publisher took the risk of bringing out the work. Kepler had to give it in commission; but one year later a German version appeared under the title: *Österreichisches Wein- visierbüchlein.*[23]

In 1618, 1620, and 1621, Kepler's great hand- book *Epitome astronomiae Copernicanae* was published in three parts. An excerpt from the dedi- cation of the first part of the work reads as follows:

[23] See Christian Frisch, Joannis Kepleri Opera Omnia, 8 vols. Frankfurt und Erlangen, Hayder und Zimmer, 1858 ff., vol. V, pp. 497 ff.

JOHANNES KEPLER:

Dedication of the first three books of Kepler's
"Epitome of the Copernican Astronomy"
To the Estates of Upper Austria

Linz, August 13th, 1617
Soon after the publication of my research on the
movement of Mars at the suggestion of friends,
familiar with astronomy, I undertook to delineate
in a compendium, the new form, which I have
given to astronomy under the auspices of the Emperor Rudolph and to present it in such way as
to make it suitable so to speak for the benches of
elementary schools. As one can learn this science
with real success only if everyone who wants to
enjoy its fruits in later manhood has sown its seed
in early boyhood, I wanted to aid everybody by an
easily understandable analysis, low price and pretty
large edition.

(Here reports follow on his difficulties with
printers, publishers and booksellers)

According to the judgment of all modern astronomers, the extraordinary hypothesis of Copernicus
deserves to be examined thoroughly and to be

made more comprehensible in all its parts. Others may take any attitude towards it they please; I take it as my duty and special task to defend it before the world (and the readers) with all the powers of my brain; for I have recognized it in my own mind as true and in contemplating it, I am filled with unbelievable delight at its beauty. But there are people who fear that by accepting the daily movement of the earth the spherical world could not be taken into account, for if . . . we say it might entirely upset the view that it is not the heavenly spheres which are moving but the earth, why then, they ask, is a sphere needed? And one can bring up many seemingly striking objections to which ordinary solutions are not always obtainable. Therefore, I thought it my duty to clear all this up in the *Epitome* (since this had never been done).

If someone wishes to accuse me, therefore, of a passion for innovation, he should know that there is no such reproach in philosophy; the whole of philosophy is an innovation as far as the old ignorance is concerned. The only thing which matters is whether one presents something new out of thirst for hankering after glory or love of wisdom. If I were greedy for glory, I think I should not lack the talent to discover something special. As to the philosophy, which I represent, however, most of it was discovered by others; though indeed, I do not present it in slavish dependence but have put it together from different authors, so that one can see how each one in his own way has acquired parts of the truth. For, as long as the multitude does not err, I want to be on the side of the many. Therefore, I take great pains to explain to as many people as possible the essence of my theory, and I am very happy whenever I can take sides with the majority. However, although a good sovereign wants peace first of all, he wants victory if he cannot have peace. In the same way, despite all the hardships caused by my deviation from the opinion of the masses, I am encouraged by the thought that in the end the bright light of truth breaks through long lasting clouds of public prejudice; and always, when I fight on the side of truth, victory is finally mine. This would not be victory unless for a long time previously there had been fighting with exertion and danger.

As by the grace of His Highness the Emperor and your friendliness I have been made priest of

God, the creator of the book of nature, I have composed this hymn for God the creator. It rather represents a new type of poetry but it tunes to the age-old and yet new lyre of Samian philosophy.

Therefore, highly noble delegates, take this small gift as duty has forced me to construct it—that is to say, carefully worked out; take it with merry countenance and protect me and my studies as you have done in the past.

In 1619, another of the masterworks of Kepler appeared, his *Harmonice Mundi* (The World-harmony). In the third chapter of the fifth book of this monumental piece of writing, the third of the three Keplerian laws is to be found; this law indicates the relation between the periodic times of the planets and lengths of their orbits. As Kepler tells us, when, after some earlier miscalculations, he finally realized that Brahe's observations really verified his own hypotheses and calculations, he first thought he was dreaming. But soon he and all later generations became aware that what he had found forms one of the basic presuppositions of any precise understanding of our planetary system.[24] It is the law stating that the squares of the periodic times of the planets are proportional to the cubes of their mean distances from the sun.

Kepler's aspirations, however, go even much higher than those of modern scientific astronomy. As he had tried to do in his *Mysterium Cosmographicum* he coupled in his *Harmonice Mundi* the precise mathematical results of his investigations with an enormous wealth of metaphysical, poetical, religious and even historical speculations. He boldly assumes that not only men but also the celestial bodies themselves have some soul or awareness of the harmonies of the universe. Further, he states, e.g., that if observed from the sun, the proportion between the wavelengths of certain planets is the same as the relation between the lengths of cords producing harmonic tones; and in this way Kepler sees everywhere realized musical, geometrical and arithmetical harmonies. As late as in the beginning of the nineteenth century, one of the leaders of German idealism, Schelling, praised in his aesthe-

[24] On the other hand, in his *Histoire de l'Astronomie Moderne,* Paris, 1821, tome I p. 360, Jean Baptiste Delambre is obviously right in stating that immediately after the appearance of *Harmonice Mundi* no one, not even Galileo, properly sensed the importance of the discovery of Kepler's three laws.

tics [25] Kepler's comparison between the perihelion, the greatest proximity of the sun, and the major key in music, the aphelion, the greatest distance from the sun, and the minor key in music; and Kepler's attribution of the various ranges of voice, such as bass, tenor, contralto, soprano and treble, to the various planets.

Moreover, to this aesthetic, poetical world view everything is in some degree animated, self-conscious, and not only dead inorganic nature mechanically regulated; Kepler also presupposes everywhere psychological harmonies connected with certain harmonic physical relations and expects marked historical events linked with excellent harmonic constellations of the planets. And yet, in his hands such speculations do not sink down to the level of superstitions, they are dictated only by adoration of the newly discovered order, the aesthetic grandeur and the intellectual subtlety of the structure of the universe. Small wonder, therefore, that the last words of Kepler's great intellectual poem on World-harmony sound almost like a psalm and a prayer. "Great is God, our Lord, great is His power and

[25] F. W. J. Schelling Werke, ed. by Otto Weiss, 1907, vol. III, pp. 150 f.

there is no end of His wisdom. Praise Him, you heavens, glorify Him, sun and moon and you planets, whatever may be the sense organ by which you become aware of Him, whatever may be the tongue by which you praise Him. Praise Him, heavenly sounds, praise Him you judges of my discoveries, especially you, Mästlin, in your blessed old age, who inspired my efforts by your encouragement and your hopes. Praise Him you, my soul, the Lord, the creator, as long as I live. For out of Him, through Him and in Him are all things, every perception and every knowledge, that of which we are profoundly unaware and that of which we know, oh, so little, in comparison with all that is beyond our reach. To Him be the praise, the honor and the glory from eternity to eternity."

The weak and melancholy astronomical teacher of Kepler, who so often in his later years kept his silence when his touchingly devoted former student entreated him to answer urgent questions, —Michael Mästlin hardly deserved such a monument of gratitude as that given to him in the passage just quoted.

In the same year, 1619, in which the *Harmonice Mundi* appeared, another work on the comets followed that of 1607, *De Cometis libelli tres,* "Three pamphlets on the Comets"; and in 1621, Kepler brought out a new annotated edition of his *Mysterium Cosmographicum* of 1596, for which he wrote the following dedication to the Estates of the Grand Duchy of Styria.

Dedication of the second edition of the *Mysterium Cosmographicum*

Frankfurt, June 30, 1621

To the Estates of the Grand Duchy of Styria

It was almost twenty-five years ago that I published the present little book, the *Worldmystery,* [see dedication of the *Worldmystery* dated May 15, 1596] and dedicated it to the body of elected men of your highly honored community. Though I was very young at that time and this publication my first astronomical venture, yet the success which it had in the following years proves that nobody has ever written at first attempt anything more significant and worthy as far as the subject matter is concerned. It would be a mistake to see in it merely an invention of my mind. Far be it from me to boast and to expect too much admiration for me from the reader, when it is our task to touch the seven-corded harp of creative wisdom. As if an oracle had dictated to me from the heavens, the chapters of the published booklet were at once valued as excellent and thoroughly true by the whole intelligentsia (something that generally seems to be the case only with the manifest works of God). To myself, working for the last twenty-five years at the reform of astronomy, these chapters have given light and guided me more than once. For practically all astronomical books which I have published since then could refer to some of the main chapters of this small book and represent a more thorough and refined exposition of them. . . . During the Civil War in Greece, Plato took the opportunity to give the people some wholesome advice and said: according to Apollo, Greece will come to peace again, only if the Greeks turn to geometry and the other philosophic studies; for these studies, he said, lead the mind from ambition and the other passions, out of which war and other evils arise, to love, peace and moderation in all things.

Now that the weapons have been laid down, if only the needs of the time would grant enough of an interval, for men of good will to find time to think out a similar plan as Cicero once did! When, after the fall of the republic, he could hardly find any consolation in his grief, when everything was lost and no hope existed of regaining the loss, and he realized that no opportunity was left for his former activity either in the *Curia* or the forum, he devoted all his energy to philosophy and also encouraged his friend Sulpicius to take up these things, as they divert the hearts from grief and lighten the sorrows, even if they are in themselves of less practical use.

If God fulfills these wishes, my mathematics will always be ready to offer delight not unworthy of a Christian, and give relief from sorrow either in the astronomical practices or in the contemplation of the heavenly works of the harmonies of the universe. (A benevolent fate has made me do this work during the sharp [political] dissonances of the last two years.) . . .

Along with these major publications, however, he produced *Ephemerides i.e.* astronomical year-books and, again, calendars with prognostications in order to secure a living for himself and his family. In the following letters he reports especially about this and the Prague salary [which the Emperor Matthias still owed him from the days of his stay in Prague and from a later grant] as well as about other difficulties with mail couriers, bookdealers, printers, paper manufacturers, assistants, and censors, difficulties which he had to overcome again and again up to the last years of his life.

To Johann Matthias Wackher von Wackhenfels, Councilor at the Court of Emperor Matthias I in Prague

Linz, beginning of 1618

Again a year has waned since you took renewed occasion to show me your benevolence and magnanimity. I want to give you an account of how I spent this year, as my silence should not give reason for the suspicion that I failed to remember such a remarkable man. Immediately after my return from Prague I took up the *Tabulae Rudolphinae* and *Ephemerides*. In order to raise the money for the *Ephemerides* of two years I wrote a cheap calendar with two prognostications; this seems at least a bit more decent than begging. Besides, in this way the honor of the Emperor is saved. He let me down completely, so that, despite all instructions recently given to the Chamber of Finance, I might have starved. The *Ephemerides* of 1618 have been printed in my new types; but it did not reach Frankfurt in time. . . . I translated the third book of the *Harmonica* of Ptolemy into Latin and added musical notes, comparing my discoveries concerning the heavenly harmonies with his views on the same subject. It is certainly appropriate that I communicate the main content to such a "harmonious" man as you are. For there is nothing in life which would give me greater pleasure. Therefore I do not wish to miss the opportunity to acquaint you with it at the present time. [Some odd remarks follow about the possibility of inhabitants of the sun. Referring to this he concludes]: If I were a heathen and had not heard anything of Christian teaching, I would say that on the sun— that excellent globe of the universe—is a place of refuge open to all brave Wackher-souls. . . . (The German *wacker* means brave in English and to apply the term wacker-brave to Wackher von Wackhenfels means, therefore, a friendly flattery to Wackher, the addressee of this letter.)

JOHANNES KEPLER:

To Octavio Pisanus in Antwerp

Linz, April 18, 1618

I received your letter of January 4th in February.
Am I in your debt that you think you must answer
my silence with a display of praise commonly bestowed only on haughty people? Did I not answer
quickly when you wrote to me in 1614? Of course
it looks as if you were rightly blaming me for my
slowness. Yet, this charge, too, will vanish if you
get to know the reasons. We here in Linz are deprived of the benefit of mail service. The couriers,
however, are hostile towards the scholars because
we pay them no more than small sums. They insist
on their demands, though we do not make any
profit out of our writing, live poorly and draw a
poor salary. If I am not mistaken they have charged
me with ⅓ gulden for the delivery of a letter. I
therefore fear, that they will not bring my letter
to Regensburg, as it often happened, or they would
deliver it badly there. So I thought it better to
await the coming *Messe* [yearly fair] in order to
accept the services of merchants without charge....

Memorandum to Foreign Bookdealers,
especially in Italy

Linz, Spring 1619

I have written this work as a German, after the
German fashion and with German frankness. The
greater the freedom of thought the more will faith
be awakened in the sincerity of those who are
devoted to scientific research. I am a Christian, a
son of the Church, and accept the doctrine of
Catholicism not only with my heart but also with
my head as far as I have been able to grasp it up
to my present age; I give proof of this in more
than one passage of my book. What else is written
in my book does not bring you any danger and can
stand the censorship in your country. . . . Only
one difficulty arises in the teaching of the movement of the earth around the sun, because of the
rough procedure of some few who have lectured
about it at the wrong place and not in an adequate
manner; this has led to the interdiction of the reading of Copernicus, until the book might be corrected
even though it has been entirely free for almost

eighty years (since the dedication of the work to Pope Paul III). . . . Though being by this time a rather old pupil of Copernicus—I have been his follower now for twenty-six years—I have only quite recently heard this about the interdiction of the Copernican doctrine. But there are men in high positions of the State and the Church who encourage the astronomers by saying the censorship did not take place and that the freedom to discuss problems of nature and to elucidate the works of God would not be squelched even by censorship. Though the die be cast already or danger lie ahead, I must openly confess a guilt. Having hesitated far too long with the publication of my works, I let it happen that the new philosophy remained undefended. . . . For indeed, if I am entitled to have any opinion at all, even the most learned among the Italians and philosophers and the most ardent amongst the theologians will have to say after having read this work on harmonies: the sublimity and fineness in the harmonious order of the divine work is so great, that Copernicus could not possibly have been understood sufficiently before the publication of this work. Therefore philosophy requires and Copernicus asks for the favor of being entirely replaced in his right . . . without hurting the honor of the judges; he . . . asks them to open a new proceeding and to examine newly available evidence which has not been understood up to the present day through carelessness of his advocates.

You bookdealers, it is true, will act according to law and order, if, considering the given judgment, you will not openly offer copies of my book for sale. But you must realize that you have to serve philosophy and the good writers, so to speak, as "notaries," who must provide the judges with the written defense. Therefore, please, sell the book only to the highest clergy, the most important philosophers, the experienced mathematicians and the profoundest metaphysicians, to whom I, personally, as the advocate of Copernicus have no other approach. These may decide whether it is only the fabrications of an eccentric imagination which are at issue or whether it is something which can be verified by evident facts as the result of the investigation of nature. These men may decide whether one should make these immeasurable beauties of the divine works known to the common people or rather diminish their glory and suppress them by censures. And as the theologians have requested the improvement of Copernicus' teaching from the scholars, they themselves may judge whether . . . the harmonious construction of the heavenly movements, as it is interpreted in my present book, can exist at all if one sets aside the movement of the earth and accepts that of the sun. The theologians may decide which of the two hypotheses confronted in the title page of Book V—that of Copernicus or that of Brahe—should henceforth be regarded as valid (the old Ptolemaic is surely wrong). Whatever the decision may be after all the reasons are objectively examined, the mathematicians belonging to the Catholic Church will doubtless acknowledge it [the Copernican hypothesis] as legitimate and unassailable.

To Vincenz Bianchi (Count Alerani) who informed Kepler in January 1619 that an "outstanding mathematician" preferred Kepler's theories to those of Brahe and Ptolemy but wondered whether he would live long enough to see Kepler's *Rudolphine Tables* appear.

To Vincenz Bianchi

Linz, February 17, 1619

. . . The philosophy which has conversed with me in middle-class dress up to now, has put on a stately costume, after having recognized the aristocratic position of the man with whom she wants me to have intercourse. A certain pride was aroused in me, too, through the Emperor Sigismund. I have heard this about my ancestors: one of my forefathers, Heinrich, and his brother Friederich were knighted in Rome in the years 1430 on the Tiber bridge, having accompanied the Emperor along with other Swabian knights. But need impelled my closest ancestors to become merchants and workers during the last hundred years. Consequently the documents were neglected and finally lost, till in 1564, Maximilian II made out an acknowledgment to my grandfather in rather general terms. . . .

I see you are reproaching me for delaying my forthcoming works. I am therefore sending you a copy of that part of Book III of the *Harmony* which has so far been printed. . . . If danger arises and the censors present difficulties, write me in detail about it; I urgently ask you to do so. . . .

JOHANNES KEPLER:

As far as the delay of my work is concerned, I have many reasons for excuse. First of all, I cannot be made responsible for the precarious conditions at the Court of Rudolph, the disorder in the kingdom, and my domestic misfortunes which have handicapped me for many years. Of these difficulties, the worst one is that, although I have been granted a rather honorable allowance by the Emperor, it has never been paid. If I did not receive a small income from the Estates of this country, I could not even meet the expenses of my household but should have had to ask for foreign help a long time ago, much to the disgrace of the Prince. Consequently, I can rarely hire an assistant mathematician. I have at present an industrious arithmetician and an expert in the whole field of mathematics, Gringalletus from Savoy. He could spend many years at my home calculating the ephemerides. But, since the Emperor has failed me, I cannot pay him sufficiently and I am not at all sure whether he will stay on. Then everything will again fall on my shoulders. Often I do not even find time enough to write letters to my friends, not to mention the carrying out of the calculations. Certain reasons for the delay are also caused by my nature.

"None of us can do everything." I cannot submit to strict order, I cannot bind myself by deadlines and I am irregular. If something orderly is produced by me it has been worked all over ten times. Sometimes an arithmetic mistake, made in a hurry, holds me back for a long time. I could pour out ever so much. For, even though I lack pleasure in reading, I have ample imagination. But I do not like myself in such a topsy-turvy state; it is repulsive to me and makes me ill-tempered. I therefore throw the material away or keep it till I can examine it again, that is to say till I write something new, which is generally the case. I also beg you, my friends, do not condemn me entirely to the treadmill of arithmetical calculations, but leave me some time for philosophic speculations, which are my only delight. In the introduction to Book V of the *Harmony* I have not concealed the fact that some people are cross with me because of the delay of the *Rudolphine Tables*; they said that I had "wasted" my time with philosophic speculations. Everyone has likes and dislikes of his own. Some like the Tables and Nativities; [26] I prefer the flower of

26 That is, lists of the positions and movements of the celestial bodies and prophecies of human fate on the ground of these positions.

astronomy, the artful structure of the movements. However, the *Tables* themselves have produced many causes for delay. I do not want to talk about the difficulties. The form of arithmetic already completed must be entirely worked over with the logarithms, so that somebody making use of my basic ideas can have a much more convenient method at hand in the future. And finally, even if the *Tables* were ready, publication could still be prevented by Brahe's family; for since it is through their permission that Brahe's observations are in my possession, I am under obligation towards them.

To Quietanus Remus, physician at the Court of Matthias I in Prague

Linz, August 4, 1619
. . . I am still in Linz, more by force of circumstances than by free will, in the midst of the present chaos. I hope I am well sheltered by the prestige of my innocent studies, and, in case something happens, by the protection which you grant your friend in Urania. I could produce more, yet the time is

unfavorable. With your letter I received the first piece of news about the banning of one of my books in Rome and Florence. I do not quite understand which book you call the Copernican. For all my books are Copernican; including the *Prolegomena to the Ephemerides*. The *Harmony* has not yet been published; perhaps one of the title pages of the Book V, which I sent you, did get to Rome and did fall under censorship there. Yet I think that you mean the *Epitome Astronomiae Copernicanae*. I will give the postmaster a copy of this edition, which I bought from the bookseller for 30 kreutzer (in Strassburg it is sold for 80 kreutzer) unless he refuses to accept this parcel. I beg you with all my heart to send me a copy of the wording of the verdict, and to let me know whether the censorship of the book would be of disadvantage to its writer in case he were in Italy, and whether he could be forced there to denounce the book. I would also be interested in knowing whether the book would be forbidden in Austria. For, if this were so, I should not only be unable in the future to find a printer in Austria, but also the copies left, according to my wishes, in Austria by the salesmen who repay the costs would be endangered, and the loss would be mine. Yes, one will have me renounce the vocation of an astronomer after I have almost become an old man in defense of the Copernican teaching without having suffered any contradiction thus far. In the end I should also have to renounce Austria, if she no longer had any room left for the freedom of philosophy. . . .

Quietanus Remus to Kepler

Vienna, August 13, 1619
The *Epitome* will soon be sent directly along to Galileo with a letter of his Highness. . . . Your *Epitome* can be read in Rome and the whole of Italy with special permission by learned people and anybody who has some training in this science. Therefore there is no reason for fear, either from Italy or Austria. Only you must confine yourself to your limits and control your feelings.

To Quietanus Remus

Linz, August 31, 1619
. . . that I did not answer your letter immediately was due to my publication of the *Ephe-*

merides, the printing of which gave me more work than it did to the printer, though I have my own type plates with me at home. Further trouble was caused by the dispatch of the copies to Frankfurt. I sent three sheets of the book in advance. The other day I took the fourth sheet with me, the moment it was dry from the press. When I reached the ship, two miles from here, I found my copy baptized overnight by Jupiter. I needed three days to dry and register them, during which time we reached Aschach. Finally (so that you may have something to laugh about) the third day was entirely spent in driving away several companies of lice which had attacked me on the boat overnight. . . .

The printer granted me one hundred copies of my *Harmony* under the condition, that I would neither give them away nor sell them at a lower price than he himself is selling them.

In 1617 and 1620, however, along with all this toil and these disappointments, a special honor was twice bestowed on Kepler. In 1617, he received a call to the University of Bologna and in 1620 an invitation to come to England, though the latter invitation was less official than the former one. But in neither case could the astronomer, who was approaching the age of fifty, make up his mind to leave Germany and live as a foreigner in countries which, at that time, were extremely distant lands. The following are the letters which he wrote on these occasions, and judged in the right historical light, the reasons which he gives for his negative decisions can in neither case be considered as mere pretexts.

To Johann Antonius Roffenius, Professor of Philosophy in Bologna

Prague, April 17, 1617

I received your letter of March 1st in duplicate. Its content made me very sad because of the death of the excellent Professor of Mathematics [at your university], J. A. Magini, my intimate friend. (For all eternity may he rejoice in the triumphant choir of the heavenly souls!) In another respect, your letter honored me most highly in offering me his successorship in Bologna, the metropolis of all the universities of Europe—Bologna, which is indeed the mother of science, and which I specially esteem and admire. With this offer you have shown me your special devotion, even though you have never seen me, and you have wrapped your account of the matter itself in so many beautiful words, as suits the meaning of your favor. I have decided that as soon as I am granted an audience with His Majesty, I will submit your notification, *i.e.* the notification from the University of Bologna, and will state your desire. But I do not want to keep my real point of view in this matter from you, in using the Emperor's sickness as a pretext for delay and I do not wish to give the impression of slighting your noble intention to promote me, or of keeping you in suspense on your request by clever calculation. I am a German by origin and trained in their way of thinking, nourished by German habits and bound to them . . . by marriage . . . by ties of life, so that even if the Emperor gave his consent, I could only with the greatest difficulties transplant my living quarters from Germany to Italy. I feel tempted by the honor linked with this highly renowned place, the venerated professorship of the University of Bologna; and I am certainly attracted by the chance of getting a larger audience and a better position, and privately because of the financial advantages. Yet the period of life has passed when

one feels stimulated by new circumstances and
longs for the beauties of Italy or the promise of its
long lasting enjoyment. Added to this, as a German
among Germans I have enjoyed since early youth
a freedom in manners and speech whose use, if I
went to Bologna, might easily involve me in dis-
credit if not in danger, cause suspicion and expose
me to the denunciations of injudicious people. I
hope you will therefore not mind my comparing
of the past with what the future might bring, and
my adopting of perhaps a superfluous precaution.
If now, as before, valuable German work will get
its reward on the Emperor's order, you will understand that this means so much to us, that no soldier
tempted by the fortunes of war, nor any scientist
tempted by high promises would leave his place if
the Emperor disapproved of it. And yet I hope
that your extremely flattering call will have some
advantage for me and will cause the treasurer of
the Emperor to fulfill his wish to help me more
quickly than ever, so that I may soon publish the
Rudolphine Tables and the *Ephemerides,* the draft
of which you have already known for several years.
You and your authorities should therefore not
regret your offer, though unsuccessful at the mo-

ment. If in the future you need my help in any way, please let me know, so that I may have an opportunity to show my gratitude to you and your flourishing university.

Farewell.

Given at Prague, the 17th of April 1617 of
the common calendar.

To Matthias Bernegger

Linz, August 29, 1620

Your letter reached me at the same time as the city of Strassburg's rich gift of honor. It arrived by a strange and—in the midst of the present imbroglios—rather exceptional route. The courier of Aschach gave your letter to one who met him, as he had to go on in another direction, that courier again gave it to another till in the end it reached me. . . .

Mr. Wotonius [27] has shown great friendliness

[27] Sir Henry Wotton (1568–1639), English diplomatist and poet who was much interested in science. From one of his letters to Francis Bacon we learn that he promised Bacon to send a copy of Bacon's *Organum* to Kepler. Wotton had met Kepler in Linz where he witnessed some experiments carried out by Kepler. (See Sidney Lee in *The Dictionary of National Biography*, 1900, vol. 63, pp. 51, 55).

towards me; he regretted that he had to continue his journey so hurriedly. He told me to come to England. Yet I do not think I ought to leave this second home of mine, especially now, when it is suffering so much insult, unless I would be more ungrateful by becoming a burden to my country. Yet to decide this, must be up to the country itself. . . . At the present time, I am busy printing my four books on the theory of the heavens; the first of these books . . . contains the physics of the heavens. As a writer I have to go through far more toil in writing than all my readers will have to stand afterwards; but I also earn more joy thereby than all the prospective readers together.

In the last decade of his life, however, which Kepler entered in 1620, he was beset by far more disquietudes than could be outweighed by the few honors done to him. After Duke Maximilian of Bavaria had conquered Linz in July 1620, the Protestant rule in the city was broken; a growing oppression of Protestants began, similar to that which Kepler had already experienced more than twenty years earlier in Graz. The following letters give an impression of the conditions prevailing in

Linz and Styria in these later years of his life, after he had published his logarithmic tables *Chilias logarithmorum* (1620), his edition and revision of Tycho Brahe's *Hyperaspistes* [28] (1625), and had prepared a book on the moon which could be published only after his death by his son Ludwig under the title *"Somnium, seu opus posthumum de astronomia lunari"* (1634) [29] (Dream about the Astronomy of the Moon).

To Peter Crüger, Professor of Mathematics in Danzig

Linz, February 28, 1624

. . . Mästlin used to laugh about my endeavors to reduce everything, also in regard to the moon, to physical origins. In fact, this is my delight, the main consolation and pride of my work, that I succeeded in that. . . .

[28] Brahe's *Hyperaspistes* which contained the doctrine of the parallaxes and discussions of "New Stars" was published by Kepler in 1625. Kepler revised Brahe's book and furnished confirmations of its thesis.

[29] See Christian Frisch, Joannis Kepleri Opera Omnia, 8 vols., Frankfurt und Erlangen, Heyder und Zimmer, 1858, vol. VIII, p. 27 ff.

I add the *Prognosticum* and the *Calendar* for this year. [Kepler had already published *Prognostica* in 1604, 1618, 1619, 1620.] I beg you, to read the introduction (and convince yourself that this dedication concerns something honorable). And imagine that the delegates of Styria have really burned all copies publicly in the presence of my mandatory. I will fall dead if even after you have put every word to the rack, you find one conclusive argument for which I should suffer this affront. . . .

To Paul Guldin, Jesuit Father, Professor of
Mathematics in Vienna

Linz, December 10, 1625
At last on the 4th of December, I received twenty-three copies of the *Hyperaspistes,* ten copies of the *Chilias logarithmorum* and two copies of the Supplement. Though your Reverence wrote you had bought a copy already, nevertheless, I want to send five copies of the *Hyperaspistes.* One copy, which had fallen apart and which was sent to me from Ulm previously, you have, I hope, received through the kindness of your society [the Jesuit order]. The people of Linz paid me for it in beer, which they tendered me without charge. . . .

Up to the present day the difficulties with the printing continue. . . . Apart from other drawbacks, I am threatened with the possibility of being expelled at the next opportunity from the house of the diet in which all delegates, including the clergy, unanimously granted me an apartment. I can hardly tell you what loss of time this would cause me, as it would throw my files entirely in disorder. I beg your Reverence to support me in case this affair is mentioned one day.

To Paul Guldin

Linz, February 7, 1626

. . . That I cannot send the two books by Snellius is due to the fact that the Commission of Reformation, by order of the dean and secretary who were in charge of the removal of heretical books, sealed the books of all the inhabitants of the house of the diet. Therefore, my whole library has been sealed up since January 1st, with the exception of a very few books. To regain the books they set the condition that I myself should select those which are to be surrendered, that means that the bitch must surrender one of her young ones. The mark of such slavery burns! Therefore, I would rather be present as a spectator and render account when they themselves name the books. As I have only a few books, there is almost none among them which would not deprive me of the fruits of my studies if taken from me, because of the various notes and comments I made in them. I have only three Calvinistic books; but I myself have written against them, partly in special copies, partly in remarks in the margin. Among them is a Greek edition of the New Testament in folio which I do not want to lose at any price because of the variants of the text given in the volume; the notes and translation, I think, are trash, and as mentioned before, I have effaced the Calvinist remarks, by crossing them out. The same is the case with the German Bible in Luther's translation; if nothing else, the chronological notes are of indispensable help to my memory. I have a single postil by Brenz [30] which I

[30] Johann Brenz (Joannes Brentius) (1499–1570), born in the same town as Kepler, one of the most influential fathers of the Lutheran Church especially in Swabia but also in other parts of Southern Germany. The postil which Kepler mentions is probably Brenz, *Postilla, Auslegung der Evangelien*, Frankfurt, Egelnoff, 1554, or one of the later editions of these once famous commentaries on the Gospels. The woodcuts of these editions published by

love for its beautiful woodcuts. The other day I spoke with Father Keller about the matter. I hoped he would intervene on my behalf out of regard to your Reverence. But to my distress, I found him harsh and inaccessible. He was, however, more friendly when we parted than when I came to him. He said that he had heard I had given secret lessons. . . . Even if I would offer to teach, no one would listen to me. . . .

If I could only obtain soon the observations on the eclipse from India or from any other place (where it occurs). . . .

I place all my hope in your benevolence, in that of the promoter of science. I close with friendly regards.

To Wilhelm Schickard, Professor of Hebrew
in Tübingen

Linz, April 25, 1626
I wish you could watch and see what is happening here, so that you might prepare your mind for

---

Egelnoff were mainly works by H. S. Beham, Hans Weiditz and Konrad Faber, see Walther Köhler. *Bibliographia Brentiana*, Berlin, 1904, p. 301 and *Allgemeines Lexikon der Bildenden Künste* ed. Ulrich Thieme und Becker, Leipzig, 1914, vol. X, p. 369.

similar troubles when one day the time of trial comes for you. . . . It is a great comfort that we are not burned, but allowed to live, if there is any meaning in the permission to live for him who has been deprived of the necessary means of life. As I hear, the minors, the peasants and the workers have not been allowed to leave the country except with the entire loss of their possessions and honor, at least within the country; for abroad one cannot touch a man's good name. But this does not apply to me. For, so far, I have been allowed the privileges of a courtier. . . .

In the present confusion not only in Germany but also in most other countries of Europe, don't be astonished that my plans concerning the edition of the tables were affected by this disorder and had to be put off for the present. I am just as anxious for the publication of the tables as Germany is for peace, and I do not take less trouble about it. But I have not made any headway either.

Nevertheless, in the midst of all the turbulent events of this first period of the Thirty Years' War, Kepler kept his serenity of mind, especially in everything concerned with his work. Thus he writes

To Matthias Bernegger

Linz, December 4, 1623

Two years ago, immediately after my return to Linz I have started to work again on the astronomy of the moon, or rather to elucidate it by remarks. I am still waiting in vain for a Greek copy of Plutarch, which though promised me has not yet been sent to me from Vienna. There are just as many problems as lines in my writing, which can only be solved astronomically, physically or historically. But what can one do about this? How few people will attempt to solve them? The people wish that this kind of fun, as they say, would throw itself around their necks with cosy arms; in playing they do not want to wrinkle their foreheads. Therefore, I decided to solve the problems myself, in notes, ordered and numbered. To this I must add an observation which I made lately through my telescope, something wonderful and remarkable: towns with round walls, as one can see by the shadows. Is there more apology needed? Campanella wrote a *City of the Sun*.[31] What about my writing a "City of the Moon"? Would it not be excellent to describe the cyclopic mores of our time in vivid colors, but in doing so—to be on the safe side—to leave this earth and go to the moon? However, what would such a flight be good for? More in his *Utopia* and Erasmus in his *Praise of Folly* ran into trouble and had to defend themselves. Therefore let us leave the vicissitudes of politics alone and let us remain in the pleasant, fresh green fields of philosophy.

Even one of the worst threats to the reputation of Kepler's family was met by him with the energy of a really great intellectual fighter. Toward the end of 1615, Kepler had heard from his sister that his mother, who lived in Württemberg in the town

[31] Thomas Campanella's *Civitas solis,* which was published first on pp. 417–464 of *Campanella's Realis philosophiae epilogisticae partes quatuor,* Frankfort, 1623, and Thomas More's *De optimo rei publicae statu deque nova insula Utopia* (1516) are leading Utopian literature of the later Renaissance which suggest political and social reform in the disguise of reports on human societies outside the globe or even the universe. According to his letter of December 4, 1623, translated above, Kepler who was probably interested in Campanella's *Apologia pro Galileo,* 1622, must have read the *City of the Sun* immediately after its appearance.

of Leonberg, was suspected and accused of witch-craft. This meant for many years of his life a veritable hell to the man completely absorbed by his intense research work and already vexed by far too many other worries.

The details of these charges against his mother show us graphically how near these times of the founders of modern science still were to the worst superstitions of the Middle Ages. In the case of Kepler's mother, the accusation of sorcery and an alliance with the devil was originally raised by a former intimate friend of the accused, the wife of the glazier at Leonberg, Mrs. Reinhold. The "Reinholdin" had once drunk a bitter herbal draught at the home of Kepler's mother; and when she later suffered from periodical fits of insanity, partly caused by bad conscience on account of some illegitimate sexual intercourse, she suspected "die Kepplerin" of having caused all her illness by having offered her a magic potion. The rumors about the witchcraft of Kepler's mother spread rapidly. The most absurd reasons were given as proofs of her pact with the devil: her restlessness, her inability to look people straight into the face, an alleged inability to shed tears, her interest in the skull of her father at the time of the opening of graves in the churchyard, and the like.

To counteract these charges of witchcraft Kepler's brother, Christoph, and his brother-in-law, both living in Württemberg, brought an action for slander against Reinhold and his wife at the court of the Town of Leonberg; only after they had done so did they inform Johannes Kepler about the matter. Reinhold, however, and his many superstitious friends—among them innumerable officials of the town—tried to prove by another suit that the "Kepplerin" was in fact a witch. The astronomer in Linz first hoped to settle the whole affair by writing a letter to the authorities in Leonberg on January 2, 1616 and by stating in this letter in very strong terms the absurdity of the charges against his mother. But he was well aware of what was at stake for the whole family if the arguments of the opponents could not be refuted at court, and he certainly did not exaggerate by saying that his "heart almost burst" when he first heard of the alleged witchcraft of his mother.

The proceedings dragged on. During the years 1617-1620 Kepler wrote numerous detailed petitions to the Duke Johann Friedrich of Württemberg and the Vice Chancellor Faber concerning the charges against his mother, for she had been exposed to mistreatment, as well as several assaults on her life, in consequence of the charges. Kepler also travelled from Linz to Württemberg and stayed there for some time; his seventy-year-old mother in her restlessness went first to Ulm and then with her other son to Kepler in Linz, who, then, had to justify in detail her "flight" from the Württemberg authorities. Kepler, though financially hard pressed, had to employ and pay several counsels and lawyers. But, despite all efforts, his mother was imprisoned on August 7, 1620 in the Württemberg prison of Güglingen.

When this news reached Kepler, the faithful son left his wife, who expected another child, travelled through the war-stricken territory to Güglingen and spent almost one year there to free his mother and to save her from torture and eventual execution. Kepler's fear that, in the prison at least, official torture might be ordered was not unfounded. Another woman born in the same town as Kepler's mother, and accused of complicity with her had already left one of her thumbs stuck in the rack.

Kepler's defense of his mother, however, was

throughout all these years rendered more difficult by the fact that she herself and her children in Württemberg had often conducted her defense in an extremely clumsy way. They lost their temper when confronted with the authorities, and her son Christoph, particularly in his excitement, became sometimes a witness for the prosecution rather than for the defense. Moreover, the climax was finally reached when Christoph and Kepler's brother-in-law, a Protestant minister, afraid of being removed from his parsonage, seem to have become almost convinced that the mother was a witch.

Kepler knew, and frankly admitted in his numerous petitions to the Duke of Württemberg, that his mother had been for many years a difficult person, "garrulous," "fickle and even malicious," a real trouble maker and above all, extremely inquisitive. Unfortunately, she was unable to concentrate her inquisitive spirit on the exploration of the skies like her great son, but focusing it exclusively on very earthly gossip.

In all his extensive writing in defense of the old woman, Kepler was wise enough never to question the legitimacy of the belief in witchcraft itself. But he valiantly fought for the demonstration of the complete innocence of his mother in this respect. He could, however, not free her from her imprisonment. The Duke and the higher authorities in Württemberg seem to have been favorably touched by the vigor of Kepler's legal writings in this matter;—once he composed and submitted a pamphlet of sixty folios on the short notice of two days. But the lower officials at the court obviously wanted to demonstrate that they were not at all impressed by the fame of the learned "Imperial Mathematicus."

One of the protocols of the court states with obvious irony: "The defendant appears unfortunately accompanied by her son, the erudite mathematician. . . ." Thus at the end of September 1621, fourteen months after the imprisonment, Kepler could not prevent his seventy-four-year-old mother from being taken to the torture chamber and being required to confess. Only after the old woman had dramatically gone down on her knees, had asked God under prayers to demonstrate her innocence by a miracle, and had resolutely insisted that she would prefer death to an extorted confession of guilt, was she acquitted in October 1621. Half a year later she died. Yet, even years later Kepler found reason for combatting the rumors by which his "reputation was tortured" during the full year he had devoted to the defense of his mother.

ODYSSEY OF THE LAST FOUR YEARS

Throughout his life, Kepler had been longing for a stability which would allow him the fullest possible concentration on his revolutionary scientific work. But this principal desire was in his old age even less likely to be fulfilled than in his youth and his prime. Toward the end of 1626, life in Linz became intolerable for Kepler as it once had been in Graz. After his whole private library had been sealed up on January 1, 1626 on account of the "heretic" literature contained in it, he realized that he had prepared in vain the printing of his *Rudolphine Tables* in Linz. He writes, therefore, to the Jesuit Pater Paul Guldin in Vienna, October 1626: "It is an extremely strange fate which permanently handicaps me. Again and again, difficulties arise without any fault of mine." He had to travel to various cities to receive part of his salary still owed to him from Prague, but he could not effect payment although the Imperial Court in Prague requested these cities to pay him. On the other hand the Emperor Ferdinand II, who had granted him the title of an "Imperial Mathematicus", insisted that he print his *Rudolphine Tables* in Linz. But

Kepler foresaw clearly that this would be impossible on account of the political upheavals in the city. Therefore he goes on to say in this letter: "I must avoid giving the impression that I am nothing but a clumsy oaf or an idler or a trickster, and must no longer, as in the previous year, look around all over Germany to hire printers for my work in Linz. For everything in Linz is obviously meant for destruction."

Thus, as Kepler reported in his *Ephemerides for the Year 1627*, after having sent his wife and children to Regensburg, he left Linz on November 20, 1626, and went to Ulm on the Danube outside Austria, at that time a Free City of the Holy Roman Empire of German nationality. From Ulm, in the beginning of 1627, he writes the following letters to Bernegger which are, again, only too typical of the straits in which he found himself despite his international fame.

To Matthias Bernegger

Ulm, February 8, 1627
. . . As you wish to know how I am, you may be glad to hear that, with the help of God and his

angels, I have survived the siege for fourteen days safely. I did not starve either even without tasting horse-meat. Only a few had the same good luck. When with the approach of the imperial troops the siege became less tight, I sent a petition to the court in which I asked for permission to travel to Ulm and to take my letter-press with me. After having received this permission, I left Linz in November together with wife, children, books and chattels. On the way here I left my wife with three children in Regensburg in icy weather, I myself arrived in Ulm on a wagon laden with plates of my figures and table-work. Here they have already started to set type at my expense, but at twice as high a price as I had expected in Linz. May God grant that I do not succumb in the middle of my work!

A terrible wound has been inflicted on our country Austria, so that it seems to gasp for life. Therefore in my plans and deliberations I must prepare for all sorts of emergencies. Could you and some other well-wishers give me your advice as to where I could turn if necessary with the brood of my six children. After the *Rudolphine Tables* have been edited, I long for a place where I can teach them to some interested listeners, if possible in

Germany, if not there, in Italy, France, Belgium or England; but only if an adequate salary is available for the stranger.

To Matthias Bernegger

Ulm, April 6, 1627

I received your letter of February 13 and read it with great pleasure. It is so full of kindness that I fear there might be too much honey here and there. How much trouble you are taking in trying to find a position for me abroad! . . . For my part, I will not hasten my dismissal from the court. But on the other hand, I intend to find out the disposition toward me among the administrators by pretending to move, and asking for a two-year leave in order to lecture about my *Tables*. But whoever goes to a university with such an intention must not hope for a full professorship; whether an assistant professorship will be given to him, you know better than I do. If a good many students were there, I would take refuge in astrology, the nurse of astronomy. I should ask each student to tell me what the hour of his birth was and undertake to teach not only the means of calculating the positions of the planets but also the meaning of the signs of nature. . . . But for this I need a certain support or the generous hand of a sovereign or a town. . . .

Yet, despite all the humiliating and difficult circumstances which Kepler had to face again at the age of fifty-six, he succeeded in publishing his *Tabulae Rudolphinae* in Ulm at the publishing house of the able printer Jonas Saur in 1627. He also regulated and fixed measures for the City of Ulm by constructing the famous *"Ulmer Kessel,"* a kettle showing the exact relation of each of the measures in use to the other. In the midst of all his own sorrows for the future, however, when, as he said in an earlier letter, one was confronted in Germany with the choice between a town which was already devastated or one which was about to be devastated, he still found time to console and advise his friend Schickard on account of a minor disappointment which the latter had had at the University of Tübingen. He had been refused an academic position for which he had applied.

JOHANNES KEPLER:

To Wilhelm Schickard

Ulm, March 20, 1627

. . . If the avarice of your Treasury Department and the underestimation of your scientific work has hampered you, if you have been handicapped by those from whom it should be least expected, if you were not given even some temporary support on the grounds of your merits, or if they show appreciation to men of merits in your surroundings only by taking away from others the possibility of distinguishing themselves by studies, one is obliged to take this as a very bad omen that a sad collapse is approaching, which will strike the state and its citizens. The fear of a great danger may therefore free you from a less relevant grief. . . . As a friend I should like to give you, my friend, my advice in one word: stay for the present time in your professorship, like a kingfisher in his nest at the bank, when the storm is raging. Do not give up, but wait till perhaps a call from another place will give your life a new turn. If I were in your place, I would in the meantime win over the first winner in the contest by an eager demonstration of friendly feelings toward him and then, through him, let the senate know by a memorandum that you do not resent its vote. Yet, I would add, that as I did not apply for that position out of vanity but out of need and domestic difficulties, I would ask that one should consider my case at the next opportunity (say about Christmas) continuing my research work in the meanwhile and the instruction of youth. . . . If, then, by a friendly approach you win over all those who, in your opinion, damaged your cause, you would do away with their assumption that you had been annoyed by your defeat, and you would do away with all friction, so that you will find them more favorably inclined toward you on the next occasion. This is my opinion; but judge for yourself. You see that I do not know the circumstances in detail. . . .

In these years Kepler suffered from eczema and abscesses, as he mentioned in a letter of August 1625 and February 1627. But his main difficulties remained the procurement of financial means for his large family and finding a home where he could settle for good and devote himself undisturbedly to his work. None of these principal wishes of his were fulfilled. After having been for no more than a year in Ulm, he thought it necessary to present his *Rudolphine Tables* personally to the Emperor Ferdinand II and to remind the sovereign of the salary which the Court owed him ever since he was appointed Imperial Mathematicus in Prague. The *Rudolphine Tables* were dedicated to the Emperor nominally by the heirs of Tycho Brahe, who years before had handed over to Kepler the astronomical observations Tycho used in the Tables, as "our father had accepted Johannes Kepler in his home to assist his astronomical work because of his extraordinary talent." Kepler himself, however, added a dedication of which the following passages may be mentioned.

The Heirs of Tycho Brahe
to the Emperor Ferdinand II

The end of 1627 or the
beginning of 1628
What shall I say, most prominent Emperor, after the dedication of the work over which I have been pondering for twenty-six years, has already been written? I am like a man who travels in a boat over

which he has no command, and is, therefore, forced
to land wherever the ship goes ashore. And yet I
have quite special reasons which would move me
to steer toward the same shore, if the choice were
mine alone. I have had as patrons the predecessors
of Your Majesty, Rudolph and Matthias, blessed
be their memory. I can no longer render account to
them who gave me the order. To do so to their successor seems to me therefore the most appropriate
thing to do. . . . Indeed, what do I not owe to
him under whose reign I could finish, complete and
put into shape the *Tables* incomplete since the
death of Tycho! . . .

How carefully such a dedication had to be
phrased we may infer from a petition Kepler had
sent first to the advisers of the Emperor asking them
whether it would be appropriate to mention the
former King of Denmark in his dedications, although the present Danish king was an opponent
of Ferdinand II etc. But despite all this care, during the months which Kepler spent again in Prague
in 1628, he evidently succeeded only in receiving
a small part of the salary promised him many
years previously. However, he indicates in a letter

to Guldin in the spring of this year that he was again, as in earlier times, "molested by impetuous demands" to become a convert to Catholicism. Such a conversion would, naturally, have been of great advantage to him at the Court of this "Catholic Majesty" in Prague. But though decried as a heretic by his own Protestant coreligionists in Tübingen, Kepler never took into consideration a conversion to Catholicism. The natural and deep firmness of his superior, supra-confessional, religious convictions expressed itself again beautifully in one of his letters to the Jesuit Guldin.

Reasons for not becoming a convert
to Catholicism
To Paul Guldin in Vienna

Prague, February 24, 1628
. . . I hope to remain in the hereditary lands of his Majesty. But my feelings toward God would be of a rather questionable character if, only now, I started to become a Catholic. At the threshold of my life, I was introduced to the Catholic Church by my parents with the baptismal water . . . Therefore think thus of me, my best friend: I re-

main in the Catholic Church; but by rejecting all that which I do not acknowledge as Apostolic and thereby also not Catholic, I am prepared to renounce the reward offered to me at present, to which his Imperial Majesty has graciously consented, and to relinquish even the Austrian countries, the whole Empire, and what weighs so much more than all this, astronomy itself. I would add, also, life itself; if man could take away anything from himself that has been given him from above ... In the meantime, I cling to the Catholic Church. Even if she rages and beats, in my heart I remain united with her with a heart full of love, so far as human weakness allows . . .

But I have gone too far. For two lines I answered in as many sheets! In this you may recognize how much unrest boils in me. . . . No answer is needed to these arguments. We will take up astronomy again.

When Guldin sent Kepler a treatise by a friend to refute his religious argument, Kepler, in the most tactful, friendly way, told him that he had written a detailed answer to this treatise; however, he did not want to send it to Guldin because he wished to avoid all polemical tone in their friendship while at the same time doing full justice to his argument.

After having finally declared that he himself was unable to pay Kepler's salary in full, on account of the "enormous costs" of the war, the Emperor requested on May 10, 1628, in a special rescript, one of his richest subjects, Albert von Wallenstein, the commander of the armies, to reimburse the astronomer. Wallenstein, Duke of Friedland and Sagan, who was much interested in astrology, really tried to settle Kepler in Sagan in Silesia, a city owned by the Duke; and Kepler, at first, seems to have placed some confidence in the seemingly generous attitude of Wallenstein. Nevertheless, a letter sent from Sagan to his friend Bernegger, who had become more and more his most devoted admirer, does not sound too happy and optimistic.

To Matthias Bernegger
Sagan, March 2, 1629
The poets want to be useful and give pleasure. How much also you, highly honored man, most cherished friend, have delighted me in my solitude and unrest by your sympathy, I can hardly tell you. For it is loneliness which makes me feel oppressed

here, far away from the large cities; and letters come and go only slowly and are causing great expense. Added to this are the intrigues of the Reformation, which, though they did not hit me directly, did not leave me untouched. Sad examples were brought before my eyes of how acquaintances, friends, people of my surrounding have been ruined, and personal contact with the frightened people has been cut by fear . . .

What, if I should present you for fun with my astronomy of the moon? As we are driven from this earth, it will be useful to us as a viaticum on our wandering to the moon. To this book of mine I add the treatise by Plutarch about the face of the moon; I have supplemented some lacunae to make sense out of the whole, as this was impossible to Xylander,[32] who was not an astronomer by profession . . .

A girl of eleven years living in Kottbus prophesies the end of the world. Her age, her infantile ignorance and the number of her listeners have provided her with a faithful following.

[32] Xylander, well known editor of Plutarch's works, whose edition was still much used in the beginning of the nineteenth century, for instance by the young Karl Marx in his doctoral dissertation.

Kepler always showed himself especially consci-
entious in the education of his children. Particularly the letters he wrote from Ulm to Schickard,
with whom his son Ludwig lived while studying in
Tübingen, are partly touching and partly amusing
in their detailed but undoctrinaire supervision of
the activities of his son. Now, when Kepler lived
in Silesia a young mathematician and physician,
Jakob Bartsch, wrote him and visited him. And as
Kepler thought Bartsch a suitable husband for his
daughter he wrote to Bernegger in Strassburg from
Görlitz near Sagan:

To Matthias Bernegger

Görlitz, April 10, 1629
I have moved to Görlitz (on account of the printing of some smaller writings), 7 miles from Sagan.
While I was here I received a letter from my
family, in which there is much praise of your
high-minded magnanimity toward my daughter
. . . Be a father to my daughter in her marriage
affairs! . . . The gentleman in question (Jakob
Bartsch) lives in my vicinity and helps me with my
arithmetic. He is still a bachelor, and has postponed

marriage, waiting for the end of the Reformation in the Lausitz . . . Please, try to find out how he has lived in Strassburg, what habits he showed, how much money he used, how much hope can be put in his getting a professorship in Strassburg in case the matter in the Lausitz does not turn out well. One thing I do not like, he anchors his studies in astrology. He is also practicing medicine. If you think your report may satisfy me, please, write to him. In the first case, tell him that it is not advisable to give up medicine and to indulge only in mathematics. Further, give him hope that with my recommendation, he may live agreeably in Strassburg. Also tell him—what is most important—to proceed frankly after he has already given reasons for rumors by an open letter; he would propose to my daughter and you would, perhaps, be the bride's father; you are in the vicinity and well acquainted with her. Enough for a clever man! I am hurrying home.

For this prospective son-in-law, Bartsch, Kepler described his life during the previous year in a comparatively rosy light in the following letter:

JOHANNES KEPLER:

To Jakob Bartsch

Sagan, November 6, 1629

. . . Last year in September I (finally) arrived in Frankfurt with the *Rudolphine Tables* to announce their publication there and have them catalogued. According to my wishes, a price was fixed by the Imperial book commissioner at 3 *gulden* in Frankfurt currency, which scholars and book-dealers alike must pay in cash.

After having completed this business, I made an excursion to Butzbach with his Highness the Landgrave Philipp of Hesse, and spent some time inspecting the instruments and astronomical arrangements of this honorable, praiseworthy sovereign; to report about this in full would lead too far afield and would be out of place here. . . .

From there, I returned travelling slowly down the Rhine, through Württemberg to Ulm, where I had to settle some business. After that I went to my family in Regensburg in November; in December I came to Prague and presented there personally some copies of the *Rudolphine Tables* to the Emperor Ferdinand II, as they were dedicated to him

. . . At the glamorous court of the victorious Emperor, I found unexpectedly many sponsors and admirers. Thanks to their recommendations, I had good luck and success with my work, was found worthy of the abundant generosity of His Majesty, and found favor in the eyes of Count Albert of Friedland and Sagan, the generalissimo of the imperial troops—a favor I had heretofore regarded with suspicion. He is not only a hero but also a great admirer of mathematics and, thanks to these twofold gifts, almost a second Hercules, very devoted to the Emperor; I had hardly mentioned my looking around for living quarters beyond the borders of the Imperial hereditary lands when he made this unnecessary . . . He graciously assigned me a quiet place in Sagan, granted me a yearly allowance consonant with his general splendid demeanor and also promised me a printing press with the full consent of the imperial entourage.

After a sojourn of a little less than half a year at the Imperial Court, I returned in May to Regensburg in order to fetch my family; in June I went to Linz to see my former sponsors, the Assembly of Austria below the Enns. They also agreed to my leaving for Sagan and paid for the copies of the

book which I had written during many years with
a honorarium which I had never expected from a
country so gravely stricken. After having completed
my affairs in that country, I came to Prague in July
where I met my family . . . and arrived at last in
Sagan on July 25th . . .

But it is time that we remember what made you
approach me. You said you want to devise an in-
strument which, when set in motion, will show the
real causes and ways of the celestial bodies. This is
why, as you say, you have thrown yourself into the
very troublesome task of calculating the ephemerides for one year.

A praiseworthy task of noble intentions! These
intentions suit your age and your industry well
. . . ; yet it is more my business to publish ephemerides which have been calculated by myself on the
ground of the *Rudolphine Tables* published last
year.

For the moment, I want to talk with you about
what, in my opinion, is expected to be done by the
scholarly world. Even if you are the first who enters
the race, there are others who are . . . fully prepared to do the same . . . surely there are many
of whom I have not even heard, Italians, French,

Belgians and Englishmen who after having received the much desired copies [of my *Rudolphine Tables*] have taken up the same noble work of gaining fame by making them (the ephemerides) accessible for general use. I congratulate you all, as many as there are, on whatever shores you live, that you have trained your minds thus far by the study of mathematics, which alone is able to satisfy the mind by its incredible precision; . . . I also congratulate myself on the success of my publication; because it has awakened the scientific interests of mankind . . .

Therefore I owe you, my dear Bartsch, and the others who did something similar, very many thanks: you have forestalled the mean endeavors of my envious rivals . . . Looking through the catalogues of the books published in the fall, I already perceived a sheet-lightning in the distance announcing rain from the South and thunder from the West across the seas. There is Claramontius Caesennas, who is writing a book in which he has been threatening my work, for the last five years. The Englishman Robertus de Fluctibus [33] writes

[33] Fludd, Robert (1574–1637), English theosophist and physician, mainly influenced by Paracelsus. His *Monochordium*

against the Frenchman Fr. Marinus Mersennajus.[34] The latter of these two was throwing himself on the former about three years ago and, in doing so, was holding tight to my hair; it is hardly possible therefore that the former will not make his defense redound to my disadvantage . . . as he has already chosen me for his special adversary. Yet, as far as I am concerned, these people may do whatever they please . . .

We both are only human beings, the ship of the state is shaken by dangerous storms and no vessel has a safe anchorage; therefore, we also have no one who could guarantee the success of the planned edition. Each one, therefore, should determine for himself what amount of work he can undertake and on which hope he will depend.

You, my dearest Bartsch, in God's name take up the immense task with a firm grip, with a strong mind, with confidence in the future, and put your Saturn as watchman in front of your door. May he keep away all faint-heartedness.

---

mundi symphoniacum in which he attacks Kepler appeared in 1622.

[34] Mersenne, Marin (1588–1648), French theologian and scientist, intimate friend of Descartes whose correspondence with the famous French philosopher is of special importance.

When the storms are raging and the shipwreck of the state is frightening us, there is nothing nobler for us to be done than to let down the anchor of our peaceful studies into the ground of eternity.

Sagan in Silesia, in my own printing press,
November 6, 1629

Again in a letter from Sagan, Kepler is mainly concerned with his prospective son-in-law:

To Matthias Bernegger

Sagan, February 15, 1630
For a very long time I have been wanting to write to my people, as I believed they were on their way. But as the postman who left Lauban the 3rd of December returned to me only on the 15th of February, and, among other personal things, has told me of the public unrest around you and of the numerous imperial troops which are stationed in Württemberg for the winter, I am wondering whether our Bartsch could have dared to start on the dangerous road to Ulm with his prospective wife. . . .

Please make exact notes on what you spend for the support of my daughter. I will see to it that you suffer no loss. I want to equip her with all means and every possible credit . . .

Finally, after the main difficulties and delicate misunderstandings were overcome, Bartsch's marriage with Susanna Kepler took place in Strassburg in March 1630 under the care of Bernegger; and this is Bernegger's glowing report of the celebration to Kepler:

Matthias Bernegger to Kepler

Strassburg, March 22, 1630
May God turn this into our salvation and blessing; today our newly married couple, your daughter and son-in-law plan to start on their way to get to you at last. . . .

I myself, according to your wishes, have in a way substituted for you, supported by your excellent brother, Christoph and your son Ludwig. Protection and ornament to the bride in attending her were your sister Margaret and your cousin, the wife of Dr. Marchtrencher, both most honorable matrons . . . All in all, the bridal procession was made up of notable men and women of all ranks, the elite of the whole town. Consequently, I have seldom seen so many people gathered together. Everywhere the streets through which we went were crowded. The large number of spectators who streamed in, might have filled a pretty large town. But do not think for a moment that this honor was given only to the bride and the groom. It was meant especially to honor you. How much we have wanted to see you here in the flesh! But as we were not allowed to enjoy your presence, we have looked with great joy at you at least as represented in your relatives and images, in the bride, your daughter, who, in the escort of the women, shone forth like the moon among the smaller stars, in your brother, your sister and your son. The people pointed to them with their fingers and explained to each other who they were. After the ceremony in the church, we were offered a meal catered as luxuriously as the times allowed. The high Magistrate of the city had contributed two pails of exquisite wine . . . Nothing was missing to complete the gaiety except the music which has been silenced for some time now in order not to imitate Hannibal and laugh while others shed tears over the public calamities . . .

I congratulate you with all my heart on such a son-in-law and such a daughter. You could not wish for better ones.

At the same time, as Kepler's eldest daughter married in Strassburg, another daughter was born to him in Sagan in the year of his death. He writes about this and his work in the following letter to Professor Philipp Müller, the teacher of his son-in-law in Leipzig.

To Philipp Müller, Professor of Mathematics,
Botany and Medicine in Leipzig,
teacher of Bartsch

Sagan, April 22, 1630

Just recently returned from Gitschin,[35] I have been kept very busy in consequence of the confinement of my wife and the baptism of my little daughter . . .

[35] Gitschin (Jičin), town in north-eastern Bohemia. Wallenstein owned it in the 17th century and made it capital of the Duchy of Frydlant (Friedland).

My workers were handicapped by my absence. Instead of the *Ephemerides,* they therefore printed the *Astronomy of the Moon* with annotations; six sheets are ready now. In addition, there will appear a new translation of Plutarch's writing on the *Face of the Moon.* But this small treatise will be printed only during intervals of the work on the *Ephemerides.*

After the marriage ceremony, Bartsch with his wife left for Frankfort . . . Would you please ask him urgently to come as speedily as possible to Sagan with his wife to attend the baptism of my little daughter, and to remind his wife of the christening robe which she wove with her own hands in Ulm as a special gift to my wife. It is urgent; if it pleases God, the ceremony will take place the 24th of April . . .

Again family joys are described in a letter:

To Matthias Bernegger

Sagan, May 6, 1630

At last my son-in-law and my daughter have come to me. They brought me your letter with the lively description of the double feast. Placing the crown on all your kindness, you have adorned it with such oratorial elegance that I could inwardly experience what I could not see with my own eyes as if I were present. There is a saying by a comedy writer: unhappiness at home surpasses all tears. Applying this to something joyful, I see that your kindness is too great to allow me to express my joy about it as much as my heart feels it and your kindness deserves . . .

And now to your wife and her little daughter Susanne, I send my best wishes along with those from my little daughter Anna Maria, only a few days old, and her darling mother. She especially sends her warmest thanks to your wife, who was willing to substitute for her if giving birth had not hindered her just as it prevented my wife from receiving the young couple befittingly and from preparing an after-wedding feast. My son-in-law, Bartsch, is so tired from his journey that, instead of writing himself, he needs the help of my hand to add greetings to you and your family.

However, the joy over the marriage of his eldest daughter and the birth of his last child Anna Maria seem to have been the last happy events in Kepler's life. As early as in 1629, doubts must have arisen in Kepler whether Wallenstein—any more than the Emperor himself or the German cities to which the Emperor had transferred the payment of his salary—would ever pay the 11,817 *gulden* which the Court had owed him for so many years. Wallenstein had other plans with the astronomer. He wanted him to become professor of mathematics, astronomy and astrology in the University of Rostock on the Baltic Sea, after Wallenstein had become Duke of Mecklenburg and patron of Rostock University.

But for many reasons Kepler felt rather disturbed by the call which he received from the university of Northern Germany. Having lived almost sixty years in the South of the German Empire, like many other Germans of that time he obviously was not too much attracted by the more "barbaric" North. He even did not feel properly at home in Central Germany, in Sagan. As he writes to Bernegger on July 22, 1629, "I feel to be here only a guest and foreigner, almost unknown, not understanding the [Silesian] dialect and looked on as a barbarian . . . I do not possess there a house nor do I have a seat in the church as I am going my own way in my religious convictions. Who is everywhere is nowhere, in any case, he is not at home."

In Sagan, as in his earlier residences, Kepler felt at home mainly in his studies. As neither "the ship of the state" nor any other vessel of an individual had any "safe anchorage" in these stormy times of the Thirty Years' War, he tried, as he had written to Bartsch, "to let down the anchor of his peaceful research work into the ground of eternity." For, as he had said already in an earlier letter, "if there is anything that can bind the heavenly mind of man to this dusty exile of our earthly home and can reconcile us with our fate so that one can enjoy living—then it is verily the enjoyment of . . . the mathematical sciences and astronomy."

In Sagan Kepler completed a supplement to the *Rudolphine Tables* (1629), the *Admonitio ad astronomos* (about the movements of the planets for 1631), the *Epistola ad Terrentium*—a treatise containing and commenting on the observations made in China by the Jesuit Terrentius, who had expressed interest in Kepler's work in 1623—and the *Ephemerides of the Years 1621–1636* which had been brought to a conclusion with the assistance of

Jakob Bartsch. But the first joy over Bartsch, the son-in-law, soon, too, changed into comprehensible disappointment, as a letter to Bernegger of the end of October 1630 vividly shows despite all its restraint and resigned irony.

To Matthias Bernegger

Leipzig, October 31, 1630

. . . My son-in-law has returned the *Synopsis* to me; he says it can't be printed unless it is rewritten in a different way; that it would be of no value to anyone unless it were interpreted. I think he would say the same concerning Euclid, Pappus, Apollonius and Alhazen. For he has no patience in reading these writers. He could print the manuscript in question during my absence in the printing office in Sagan, if he wanted to. But I think they prefer to wait till I have returned.

. . . On the 14th of October I arrived in Leipzig. I have found a home there with my second Bernegger. He is Philipp Müller and is licentiate of medicine and professor. Now I am about to leave for Regensburg and Linz and from there to the Duke, that is to Sagan, if God will.

May you, your wife and children keep well. With me keep fast to the only anchor of the Church, the prayer to God . . .

This is the last letter which has been preserved from Kepler's hand. Kepler had not dared to decline the call from the University of Rostock, as the call had originated with Wallenstein, his protector at Sagan. But he had tried to postpone acceptance, and coupled his agreement with the condition that the 11,817 *gulden* which Wallenstein, at the request of the Emperor, was supposed to pay him should be remitted to him. In fact, however, during the course of 1630, the last year of his life, Kepler realized more and more that Wallenstein was hardly willing to pay this sum; and even if he had been, he would, as Kepler phrased it, "have had power only over his favors but fate would have had final power over him" as well as his favors.

Kepler, however, with good reason no longer wished to place his hopes on Wallenstein's good will or good luck. He, therefore, left Sagan in the fall of 1630, to see whether he could not receive his salary from the German *Reichstag* in Regensburg, the assembly of German dignitaries who should be able to honor all the promises made to him long ago by the Emperor's Court. On horseback Kepler rode via Leipzig, where he stayed with Philipp Müller, his "second Bernegger," to the South of Germany.

But the great exertions during this trip, in the fog, slush and storms of a German November, brought him to Regensburg as a man sick unto death. He died there, after a short illness, on November 15, 1630. This last trip of the astronomer of world fame, riding through half of Germany on a worn-out jade and hunting for a salary earned many years earlier and promised him again and again, is of incomparably symbolic power.

If he had received the money long overdue, he and his family would have been able to live free from financial distress for a long time. But death obviously saved him from a last severe disappointment. The *Reichstag*, assembled in Regensburg in 1630, was far too busy with problems which seemed unfortunately more important, primarily the enforcement of the abdication of Wallenstein as the commander in chief of the Imperial Army. However, the funeral procession of the great astronomer was attended by many members of this illustrious Imperial Diet in Regensburg.

Several letters, written soon after Kepler's death, give us a few more details about his end, and about the difficulties in which he had to leave his family —a prospect which only too often had haunted his life in earlier years.

Wilhelm Schickard to Matthias Bernegger

Tübingen, November 25, 1630

I must not conceal, dearest friend, the news, even if I cannot communicate it to you with dry eyes: our mutual—alas!—former friend Kepler, a star of the first order in the mathematical sky, has passed away and rose above the horizon of earthly life, on the 15th of November, in Regensburg. He was buried there the day before the lunar eclipse; he was to observe up there directly what he has so often shown us on earth and also predicted. O, what immeasurable loss have the sciences suffered by the passing away of this incomparable man! If Bartsch, his heir, familiar with Kepler's plans and quite at home with his notes, does not carry on the research only half finished, there will be lost to posterity a paramount treasure of outstanding ideas. Who will edit the *Hipparchus,* who the notes concerning the observations?

Jakob Bartsch to Philipp Müller

January 3, 1631

. . . Yes indeed, I can hardly think of it without mournful tears in my eyes . . . least of all write about it. . . . En route! O, woe! In the greatest disorder of his circumstances! O, woe! Your, mine, our sun, the sun of all astronomers has set, and has left to his people the darkness of sorrows, of struggle and confusion . . .

When I was offered a suitable chance to go to Gitschin [35] I could, and thought I should not reject it. I wanted to learn the Prince's wish, to find out what was to be expected for the widow and the children under the present circumstances, and what there was for me to do in the printing office. Against all expectations I had to wait over fourteen days in Gitschin, and yet I have not accomplished anything I had wanted. The Prince refused to pay the expenses for the printing office in the future. I could not receive the remaining portion of the yearly

income from the bursary either. What shall I say?
With Kepler dead, everything else seems to have
died too. Yet we still hope for a gracious gesture by
the Prince . . .

From the letter of an unknown
scholar, named Fischer

                              About January 1631
. . . From your letter I learned that the rumour
has spread in your area about the death of Kepler
. . . He has gone, alas, he has gone! This heavenly
soul has gone and concluded its life on earth! I will
tell you in detail what I know of his death. During
the recent meeting of the *Reichstag* Kepler arrived
here on a skinny mare (which he sold later for two
gulden). He had been here for just three days when
a fever befell him . . . Soon it increased so that
he lost consciousness. As long as the illness lasted,
he did not talk like one in possession of his mind.
Some priests came to see him and refreshed him
with the living water of comfort. When at last he
was wrestling with death and gave up his spirit, a
servant of God, in a manly way, as it should be,
spoke to him. He was the Protestant clergyman of

Regensburg, Sigmund Christoph Donaverus, a relative of mine. This took place on November 15th,
1630. On the 19th he was buried in the cemetery of
St. Peter's, outside the town. For it is not the custom
to bury Lutherans inside the walls.

Even the grave of Kepler, outside the walls of the
city of Regensburg, did not remain untouched.
Friends of Kepler had erected there a simple stone,
carrying four lines of a verse once composed by
Kepler himself for this purpose:

> Mensus Eram Coelos Nunc
> Terrae Metior Umbras
> Mens Coelestis Erat
> Corporis Umbra Iacet
>
> Once I measured the skies,
> Now I measure the earth's shadow.
> Of heavenly birth was the measuring mind,
> In the shadow remains only the body.

Not later than three years after the funeral, the
cemetery outside the walls of Regensburg and Kepler's tombstone were completely destroyed during
the conquest of the city by the Duke Bernhard of
Weimar in the heat of the Thirty Years' War. And

it was not until about two hundred years later, in 1808, that Karl Theodor von Dalberg, Prince Primate of the Confederation of the Rhine, the friend of Goethe, Herder and Schiller, built a monument in honor of Kepler at that burial place of one of the greatest and noblest minds of modern times.

SELECT BIBLIOGRAPHY

A. WORKS CONTAINING THE LATIN OR GERMAN ORIGINALS OF KEPLER'S LETTERS:

Epistolae J. Keppleri et M. Berneggeri mutua, Strassburg, 1672.

M. G. Hansch, *Joannis Kepleri aliorumque Epistolae mutuae,* 1718.

Christian Frisch, *Joannis Kepleri Opera Omnia,* 8 volumes, Frankfurt a.M. und Erlangen, 1858–1871.

Johannes Kepler, *Gesammelte Werke* ed. by Max Caspar, München, 1938 ff. Only a few volumes of this new monumental edition have as yet appeared.

Johannes Kepler in seinen Briefen, ed. by Max Caspar und Walther von Dyck, 2 volumes, München und Berlin, 1930.

B. WORKS BY KEPLER MENTIONED IN THE PRESENT BIOGRAPHY

1595 "Calendarium und Prognosticum" for the years 1591–99 (the text of this first

199

publication of Kepler is no longer accessible either in print or among his MSS).

1596 Prodromus Dissertationum Cosmographicarum continens Mysterium Cosmographicum (Harbinger of inquiries concerning the structure of the universe and
containing the worldmystery).

1604 Astronomiae pars Optica (Optics in its
relation to astronomy, which was later
supplemented by his Dioptrice, 1611).

1605 Epistola de Solis Deliquio (on the eclipse
of the sun of October 12, 1605).

1606 De Stella nova in pede Serpentarii (The
new star in the foot of Serpentarius).

1609 Astronomia Nova (The New Astronomy)

1609 Mercurius in Sole (Mercury in the Sun
i.e. Mercurius in passing the Sun.)

1610 Dissertatio cum Nuncio Sidereo (Discussions of Galileo's "Star Herald").

1610 Tertius Interveniens (The Intervening
Third, a German writing on Astrology
addressed to Philipp Feselius).

1610 Narratio de observatis a se quatuor Jovis
Satellitibus erronibus (Treatise on the
Satellites of Jupiter).

1614 Ad epistolam Sethi Calvisii Chronologi Responsio (Answer to a letter of Calvisius).

1614 De vero anno quo Aeternus Dei Filius humanam naturam . . . assumpsit (On the year in which the eternal son of God took on human nature).

1615 Eclogae Chronicae (Chronological questions).

1615 Nova stereometria doliorum vinariorum (New stereometry of wine barrels; Österreichisches Weinvisierbüchlein).

1618, 20, 21 Epitome astronomiae Copernicanae, in three parts (Handbook of Copernican Astronomy).

1618 Ephemerides (Astronomical Year Book).

1619 Harmonice Mundi (The Worldharmony).

1619 De cometis libelli tres (Three pamphlets on the comets).

1621 2nd edition of the Mysterium Cosmographicum.

1624 Chilias logarithmorum (On Logarithms).

1625 Hyperaspistes by Tycho Brahe (revised and published by Kepler).

1627 Tabulae Rudolphinae (Rudolphine Tables).

1629 Supplement to the Rudolphine Tables.

1629 Admonitio ad astronomos (Admonition to the astronomers).

1630 Epistola ad Terrentium (Letter to Terrentius).

1634 Somnium seu opus posthumum. De astronomia lunari (Dream on the astronomy of the moon).

C. LITERATURE ON KEPLER

L. L. C. von Breitschwert, *Johann Keplers Leben und Wirken,* Stuttgart, 1831.

Sigmund Günther, *Kepler und Galilei,* Berlin, 1896.

Paul Rossnagel, *Johannes Keplers Weltbild und Erdenwandel,* Leipzig, 1930.

Hans Schimank, *Epochen der Naturforschung,* Berlin, 1930.

D. BIBLIOGRAPHICAL LITERATURE

Max Caspar, *Bibliographia Kepleriana,* München, 1936.

INDEX

INDEX

INDEX

INDEX

nia (second part of the second century B.C.), 67 and note 13, 195

Hitzler, Daniel, minister Primarius of Linz, schoolmate of Kepler, 105, 106, 111

Hölderlin, Friedrich (1770–1843), the great German poet, 24

Humboldt, Alexander von (1769–1859), world traveller and explorer, 17 and note 5

James I, King of England (1566–1625), in whose reign the "Authorized Version" of the English Bible translation appeared in 1611, 76

Johann Friedrich, Duke of Württemberg (1582–1628), 158, 159, 160

Kafka, Franz (1883–1924), the great novelist, 14

Kant, Immanuel (1724–1804), the great German philosopher, 16

Kepler, Barbara, née Müller von Mühlegg (1573–1611), first wife of Kepler, 29

Kepler, Christoph, brother of Johannes Kepler, 158, 160, 184

Kepler, Heinrich, brother of Johannes Kepler, 22

Kepler, Johannes, born on December 27, 1571, in Weil, Swabia, died on November 15, 1630, in Regensburg, from 1577–1594 educated at the Swabian schools of Leonberg, Adelberg, Maulbronn and the University of Tübingen, 22 ff.

1594–1600 professor of Morals and Mathematics in the Protestant Gymnasium in Graz, 25 ff.

1597 married to Barbara Müller von Mühlegg, 29

1601–1612 Imperial Mathematician at the Court of Rudolph II in Prague, 69

1596 *Mysterium Cosmographicum,* 30 and passim

1604 *Astronomiae pars Optica,* 69, 90

1609 *Astronomia Nova,* 37 and passim

1612–1626 in Linz, professor at the "Landschaftsschule," 105

1613 second marriage, with Susanna Reuttinger, 113 ff.

1619 *Harmonice Mundi,* 123–126 and passim

1618-20-21 *Epitome astronomiae Copernicanae,* 119–122

1621 second edition of the *Mysterium Cosmographicum,* 127–129

1627 *Tabulae Rudolphinae,* 163, 165 and passim

1626–1628 in Ulm, journeys to Frankfort, Regensburg and Prague, 164 ff.

INDEX

1628–1630 in Sagan, jour-
neys to Silesia, Lusatia,
Leipzig and Regensburg,
174 ff.

1630 marriage of his daughter
Susanna to Jakob Bartsch,
184 ff.

1630 death in Regensburg on
November 15th, 193

Kepler, Katharina (1547–1622),
Kepler's mother p. 22 accused
and imprisoned on account of
witchcraft and defended by
her son, 156–162

Kepler, Ludwig, Kepler's son
(1607–1663), physician in
Königsberg, 176, 184

Kepler, Susanna, née Reuttinger,
Kepler's second wife, 113,
116

Kepler, Susanna, Kepler's
daughter, wife of Jakob
Bartsch, 184

Longomontanus, Christian Severin (1562–1647), Danish astronomer, 66 and note 12, 92

Luther, Martin (1483–1546),
55, 113, 152, 197

Mästlin, Michael (1550–1631),
astronomer, professor at the
University of Tübingen, teacher of Kepler. Although Kepler
completely outshone his teacher's fame, his gratitude to
Mästlin never faded, 24, 27,
31, 37, 39, 43, 45, 47, 54, 55,

56, 57, 62, 63, 64, 65, 91, 106,
126, 149

Magini, Johann Anton (1555–
1617), professor of astronomy
in Bologna, 73, 144

Matthias, Emperor of Germany
(1557–1619), reigned 1612–
1617, 102, 104, 129, 140, 171

Maximilian of Bavaria (1573–
1651), Elector of Bavaria, 91,
137, 148

Mersennajus, Marinus (Mersenne, Marin) (1588–1648),
friend of Descartes, 182 and
note 34

More, Thomas (1480–1535),
156 and note 31

Mozart, Wolfgang Amadeus
(1756–1791), 19, 20

Müller, Philipp, professor of
mathematics in Leipzig, teacher of Jakob Bartsch, 186, 191,
193, 195

Newton, Sir Isaac (1642–1727),
the great English physicist,
14, 88

Odontius, Caspar, assistant to
Kepler, 92

Palestrina, Giovanni (1526–
1594), the great Italian com-
poser, 21

Pappus, Greek geometer of the
3rd century A.D., 191

Paul, the Apostle, 33

Philipp, Landgrave of Hesse, 178

INDEX